about art

Stan Berning

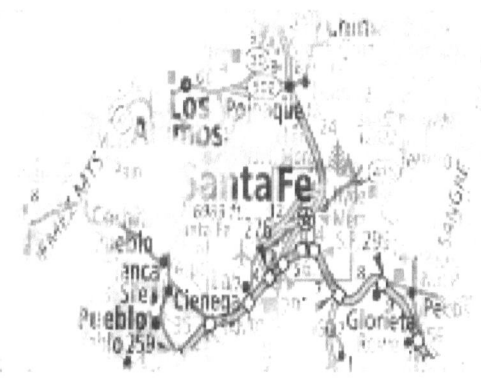

copyright 2009 by Stan Berning

Library of Congress Cataloging-in-Publication Data

Berning, Stan
about art : a novella / Stan Berning.

ISBN 978-0-578-00623-9

1. art memoir 2. artist american 3. art psychology 4. art theory 5.
art 21st century 6. travel North America 7. title

Library of Congress Control Number: 2009900577

Contents

a terrible-beautiful dream

In the street of a small rural town, surrounded by milling people, I was assisting with the lighting of candles. These candles were then placed inside translucent papier-mâché balloons. Some were no more than small paper bags clasped tightly in both hands above the head. Others were slightly larger and attached to fragile wicker frames one could uncomfortably crouch within. Once each person made the tremulous decision to ascend, they would grasp hold of these improbable contraptions and be lifted high into the air. The blue sky was soon filled with a hundred or more. Later, the candle light of each soul flickered impossibly high in a deep night sky. These pinpoints of light converged or drifted apart in random movement on the still night air; a gathering of fireflies in the complete blackness of a starless night.

With a quick tremor of fear, I thought, "The candles will soon burn out!"' No sooner had this thought come to me than the first of the lights was extinguished and the body of that soul plunged to earth. Soon more and more were falling. Two lights came together, were extinguished, and the two fell as one. From the vantage point of a bird poised just above them, I saw four who had come together. Their bodies, intertwined, fell rapidly away from me, disappearing into a foggy, obscuring blackness to perish on the desert floor far below.

Standing upon a small hill, gazing up at the few lights left flickering in the sky, I sensed with dread the bloated and decaying corpses that in the darkness surrounded us. To the man standing next to me I said, "When daylight comes there will be bodies to collect and bury."

This morning I am contemplating how we humans, awkwardly tangled in dreams of salvation, struggle to lend meaning to a physical world that is most often brutally indifferent. It may be that the one thing of substantial power left to us is our own imagination.

As a painter, I grew up seeing the world through the prism of art. As clear and true a prism as any other, art elevated me above the poverty of my everyday existence and conferred upon my life a spirit charged with potential. That potential seemed to explode onto the public stage on March 3rd of 2005 with a one-man show at New York's Lincoln Center and the premier of the film Off The Map. In this very special movie, the story of which is, in part, about a man's transformation from lost soul to artist, my paintings play a significant and pivotal role. Though I am forever grateful to the films director, Campbell Scott, for the opportunity to be a part of his exceptional project, out of it came some surprising and devastating personal consequences that left me shaken to the core and in doubt of all I had once taken for granted. Two months after its release, I sold my home and studio and, with a profound sadness, abandoned all ties to the place I'd called home for 25 years. With only the vaguest of plans and no idea of what was next required of me, I thrust myself out onto the highway in one last desperate reach for clarity.

Originally these stories, posted online at livejournal.com, were intended simply as a travel log to keep friends and family informed of my whereabouts. The writing and rewriting of them soon became an integral tool in my quest for understanding, healing, and redemption.

This is a true telling of a decisive moment upon which my world turned and, as such, it is a bridge. There will always now be that which came before and that which followed. This bridge is for my father. He never had the opportunity to make his own crossing, but through his music, despite his hard life, he bequeathed me the desire and faith to dream.

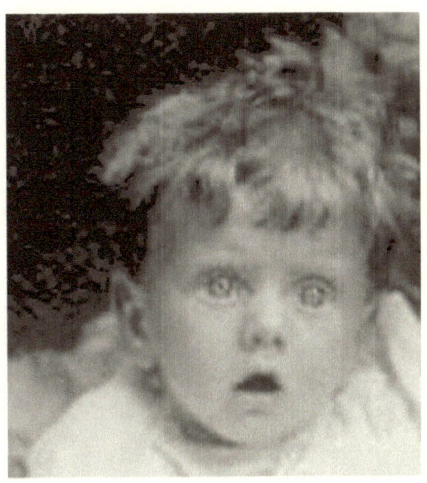

Herbert Anthony Berning
1915 - 1965

Bisbee and beyond

My dog and I have been on the road for eighteen days. The weather is cool, foggy, and quite beautiful.

The first day out from Santa Fe, New Mexico, I drove to Bisbee, Arizona. I found Bisbee unique and magical. A huge open-pit copper mine encroaches on its eastern edge and mountains of tailings surround the site for miles, but the town itself is picturesque and quite impossible to imagine. The downtown of two and three-story brick Victorian warehouses is surrounded by a series of makeshift homes clinging precariously to the cliffs of two converging canyons. Stair-steps cut into the cliffs appear and disappear in blind turns between the houses and run all the way up the canyon walls. While giving one the impression of being on an island in the Mediterranean, it is a hole in the ground in the middle of some of the hottest desert in North America. It is the kind of architecture dreams are made of. The people of the town seem open and friendly though far too familiar with each others' business, being only about 500 people. I met one genuine artist there; a woman by the name of Sam who paints like a man and loves the place.

Dixie and I stayed in a hotel that seemed ready to tumble off the cliff (not a straight floor in the place) operated by a woman who did not wish to be bothered. During dinner I overheard a conversation about the encroachment of Californians that I'd heard almost word-for-word 20 years ago in Santa Fe. The next morning, after several conversations (an actor just moved from Tucson - a local just returned from the Amazon) the heat of the day set in. By the time I reached Phoenix it was over 100. The next day,117.

I had planned to spend more time in Arizona with a stop in Palm Desert, California, but it was so impossibly hot that I changed plans and drove two hard days to get off the scorching desert floor. We landed for a time at a campground in the Los Padres mountains north of Los Angeles. There was a stream running through the site and when Dixie laid eyes on it she lost her mind, plunging in and out of the water, running madly about on a terror. She found a boyfriend, went feral for a bit and came out of the experience with ticks and an elevated sense of herself, which has rapidly disappeared since last night's bath.

I have been working my way slowly up the California coast, stopping at a number of small beaches only accessible by foot.

....

We spent last weekend in San Francisco with Howard and Joyce. It was a tough visit for Dixie, since Joyce has allergies and we had to keep her at Howard's studio. Despite all that, they were gracious as always.

My first hour with them was an adjustment after days by myself on the road. Howard is a fine painter and Joyce is the top sales person for a large art publishing house. Their new condo is absolutely beautiful, with no expense spared to make it so. It is an accomplishment to be proud of. Near the summit of Potrero Hill, they live with a view that is quite transcendent, though their hearts and minds are planted firmly in this world.

On Friday, I made a surprise visit to my gallery. Mel E was on the phone in his office while his dreadful little assistant ignored me obtusely as she always does. I stood in the center of the cavernous room, my heart pounding in my chest. Unable to catch my breath, I turned and left without a word. Later I picked up my prints at Andrea S's Gallery. I found myself very comfortable with her, rambling on about my disappointment and disgust with the business. "I'm just burnt out, Andrea. I can't do it anymore." Soon after those two visits, Howard and I had the conversation for which I had come to San Francisco.

In Bisbee I had been in a gallery that handled the paintings of a man who obviously had copied Howard's work (the tendrils, broken rectangles, and shaped canvases, even palettes). The director had bragged about having sold 90 of his paintings last year. Upon seeing some of Howard's new work I said, "This is head and shoulders above anything that copy-artist in Arizona could possibly imagine, but if you were to put this work in that space they wouldn't be able to sell it."
He replied, "Yes, I know. Isn't it amazing. I have come to the conclusion that, as a general rule, people have mediocre taste and look for things that validate those tastes. You can be too good."
"I know you'll understand this." I said "What we as painters have to offer is that 'Oh Yes!' experience when we surprise ourselves with breakthroughs and revelations. Those inspired moments are the lynchpins of all artistic experience and the only reason it has value. I always thought when I achieved that level of expertise where I could consistently elevate the dialog to find those moments, then I would be rewarded in the real world. Instead, I am finding the opposite might be true and I cannot describe the almost crippling disappointment I feel." This was the first time I'd acknowledged the toll the last few years have taken.

Later that night I lay in the dark, lost in an oversized mattress amidst a forest of pillows, listening as the sounds of the city drifted up and through the open bedroom window. In the darkness, memories of my last month in Santa Fe rolled over me with the surprising force of consecutive lightening strikes from a dangerous, too close storm.

Eight weeks before, David P, an old friend and now gallery director, having heard that I was leaving town and knowing I did not have representation in Santa Fe, arranged an interview with Rita N, the owner of the gallery where he worked. David, Rita, and I visited for two hours at my studio. She spoke at length about her spiritual work, a thing she seemed genuinely connected with, and discussed with understanding the difficulties of the business. For my part, I stayed open and curious. We were interviewing each other and for each of us the interview went well.

'Yes,' I thought with surprise as she drove away, 'I might actually enjoy working with her.' She had been charming and direct and, though I had never much cared for the predominantly mediocre tastes of her gallery, many of my friends had shown with her in the past and done well. And I had always wanted to work with David. It seemed important that, if possible, I not leave town without a local dealer.

"I've not seen enough of this new work to make an informed decision." she had said. We agreed that I would continue painting for the next month while my work-study students packed for the move.

On the last day, with the rooms empty and the walls pristine, I would do a presentation of all the work I had done.

So I spent the last month madly painting as Amy and Weston disassembled all the portions of my life and placed them in labeled boxes left scattered about me on the studio floor. There was no time for contemplation as, between those hours of submersion in the focused process of painting, the demands of the move compelled me from project to project. The movers arrived and in one ferocious ten hour surge all the chaos disappeared behind the metal doors of a storage locker two blocks to the east. As I put the finishing touches on the new paintings and prepared them for hanging, walls were patched and windows cleaned.

At 2 AM I had been scrubbing sinks and toilets, but now, at 8 AM, I stood at the center of a large empty white room, its walls as pristine as any museum's, and gazed at the twenty or so paintings hung carefully about. A pot of coffee brewed on the kitchen countertop next to bottles of wine and paper cups (later in the day I would be hosting an open house; a farewell to friends) when the phone rang.

It was David, his naturally tense voice edged with apology. "Stan, I'm so sorry, but I've overslept. I have to open the gallery and won't be able to make the meeting."

"I'm sorry to hear that, David. I was looking forward to seeing you."

"Well, Rita will be there soon. So, how goes the move? How do the new paintings look? I hope all goes well with your meeting this morning. Will I see you before you leave?"

Five minutes later he called back. The nervousness in his voice had taken a tick upwards. "Stan, I've bad news. Rita can't make it either."

On my part, a stunned silence ensued as I absorbed this information and my mind raced to register its implications.

David was saying, "..... forgot all about it. This is her day off and .....".

"What do you mean?" I interrupted. "Do you mean she's not coming at all?"

"Well, she forgot all about it, Stan, and this is her day off."

"Not at all?" I asked again. Perhaps I hadn't understood.

"No." David said. "She lives twenty miles out of town and this is her day off. She had a rough week and she says she needs to rest."

"Does she realize that this is it?" I asked, searching still for clarity. "There's no rescheduling. I'm out of here tomorrow. Does she understand this?"

"Yes, I told her. I told her you'd be disappointed. But this is her day off and she's had a rough week. She's not coming into town."

David was saying, "I'm sorry, Stan, but you know I can't tell Rita what to do. She's decided she ..." when the implications of his words overtook me.

"Do you realize how FUCKED that is?" I interrupted, and with the explosive uttering of that profanity my anger broke loose. "Do you have any idea how hard I've worked to make this happen?"

"Stan, I don't know what to say ..."

"And now you have the audacity to blow me off? HOW DARE YOU!"

"I'll be right over." David said as he turned on his dime. "I'll be right there. Just a few minutes late."

"David," I said, unmollified, "You don't have any say in who shows in Rita's gallery, do you?"

"No. No, I don't. You know I don't."

"Don't take this the wrong way, David. You know I love you but, tell me, what goddamn good does it do me then for you to come?"

During the course of this conversation I had moved from the light filled studio into the small bedroom. Naked without its furniture, no morning light ever entering its windows, I stood in its darkest corner as I heard David saying, "..... don't know what to tell you ..." and, trembling with indignation I said quietly, "Fuck you, David." and hung up.

I stood there in the sudden silence, the phone dangling from my hand, vibrating like a just struck cast iron bell.

For an hour I seethed, guttural cries of outrage and pain echoing about the hollow chamber which had once been my studio. Its emptiness now seemed a monument to this, my ultimate failure, illustrated so clearly by this last blow, this ignorant and thoughtless act of cruelty. The graphically strong paintings which, in the last month, had taken on such importance now appeared frail and of no consequence. 'One cannot care enough to make others care.' I thought. 'What a horrid lesson; to learn that no power resides in these paintings when others may simply choose to ignore them.' As the morning passed in silence the inevitability of this cruel thing Rita had done took root in my consciousness to become a metaphor for my last 25 years in Santa Fe. I asked myself, 'What have I done to deserve such terrible disrespect and contemptuous refusal from these dealers?'

By noon, though I was still shaken like a man recently beaten about the head, I found myself no longer willing to bring myself to anger. Over the course of the afternoon a steady flow of friends and acquaintances made their way up the stairs and stood about, wine cups in hand, their eyes occasionally searching the room for chairs that were not there. As the story of Rita's behavior circulated, useless words of consolation and support, varying only in tone and timber, were repeated.

"There must be some good reason she would do this, Stan." Gail P spoke placatingly. "No one could be that cruel and inconsiderate without reason. Are you sure David wasn't covering up for something more serious?" she asked.

"I wish he were," I replied "but no, I don't think so."

"Unbelievable!" Timothy N, my artist friend, ranted as he acted out his own anger.

Projecting his own difficult experiences upon the situation he exclaimed, "To hell with her, Stan. She has a crappy gallery anyway. You're better than her. Your better off without her. Who the hell does she think she is anyway? All these dealers are out of their minds. You can't trust any of them."

"Not all dealers are out of their minds, Timothy." I said, finding his tone decidedly unhelpful. "I have to ask myself if Rita has been trapped as well, drawn somehow into my own scenario of what to expect out of dealers."

"Your being way too generous." he said, and I had to agree.

Ron P offered reasonably, "The work looks great, Stan. Its too bad you couldn't get some other dealer here to see it before taking it down."

"Who would I call at this late hour?" I asked helplessly. "It's Impossible, Ron. Besides, I just don't have the strength to go through this again."

"Its too late." I added sadly. "Its just too late."

David P called late in the day. "Have you heard from Rita?"

"No." I said.

"Can I come tomorrow and see what you've done?"

"That's not necessary."

"But I'd like to see what you've done, Stan, and talk."

"There's no time, David. The work needs to come down first thing in the morning. It's final inspection tomorrow. I leave the next day."

"Can I come at 8 AM? If I come will you be there?"

And so David came the next morning. A trash bag filled with paper cups and empty wine bottles lay half full in the center of the room. The kitchen counter top was still littered with yesterday's debris.

"Has she called?" he asked.

"No, she hasn't."

"Damn, what's wrong with her?" he said, frustration in his voice. "I've told her she needs to call you."

"It doesn't matter anymore."

"Several times yesterday I told her."

A moment later he added, "I've given her my notice."

"David, don't throw your job away over this."

"I can't be a party to this kind of behavior, Stan."

"You have a good job with her. Don't throw it away over this. You have to watch out for your own future."

"I have to live with myself."

"David, not for me."

For the next hour we talked, he in the only folding chair and me atop the cooler; a sad long talk about our years in Santa Fe and the courage and cowardice with which we had each lived them. I distractedly wandered about the room as, out of obligation, he looked at each painting and tried halfheartedly to discuss them. Hearing no response from me he soon gave up. 'Its too late for that, David.' I thought as I looked out the window to the street below where I noticed Mary, his wife, asleep in the passenger seat of their parked car. An early morning for her as well.

"It's OK, David." I said as my eyes scanned the deep blue morning sky to the Sandia range, 50 miles south. "This is not between you and me. We're good."

The paintings had been loaded into the bed of my pickup truck. The holes where they had been hung were patched and painted and the cement floors had been mopped one last time. The final inspection had been successfully completed. I had spent the night on Timothy and Trisha's couch where my suitcases now awaited me. As I drove to the storage shed with this one last load of paintings, my cell phone rang. "Stan," Rita's voice spoke too close to my ear. "This is Rita. Do you have a moment to talk?"
Surprised, I replied nervously, "I don't think I have anything to say to you."
"Well," she went lightly on, "David told me how upset you are and I just wanted to apologize for not making our meeting. Last week was just so hectic and our appointment simply slipped my mind. And then I was tired and it was ....."
'This is not an apology.' I thought, and hung up.
Moments later the phone rang again. 'Shit, I don't want to do this.' I thought. But as the phone rang a second, third, and fourth time I thought, 'All right then. Let's get this over with.'
"Hello" I said as I pulled my truck to the curb.
"This is Rita."
"Yes, I know."
"I want to apologize."
Silence as I waited.

"I was thoughtless, Stan. There is no excuse for my behavior. I owe you an apology."

"Yes." I said and thought to myself, 'For what, woman? Say it out loud. Show me you understand.' Rita went on.

"I know what I did was wrong. There's no excuse for it. But I didn't intend to hurt you, Stan. It's just that I had forgotten and then I really needed a day off and ....."

"If there's no excuse then stop making them." I said with irritation.

"OK" she replied, disarmed. And another silence settled as I refused to prompt her.

Rita began again.

"I told David to explain the situation and if he didn't properly apologize, as I thought he had ....."

"Don't bring David into this. This is between you and me."

"But I told him to explain my situation and it seems he didn't ....."

"It's not his job to do your dirty work. David and I are good. He made the effort to call me back and then to come over. He made the effort, Rita. You didn't."

'And David's threat of resignation is the only reason we're talking right now.' I thought, as another silence followed. I'd had enough of this obfuscation.

The sun beat down comfortingly upon my closed eyelids as I waited, without hope, for Rita's next words. For one brief moment I expected her to hang up, but instead she spoke again.

"Stan, I promised you another look at your work.

We had an appointment and I stood you up because it was inconvenient for me. I was rude and inconsiderate but, please believe me, I didn't intend to hurt you."

'These are only words.' I thought. 'These words are cheap. They have no value. This is not nearly enough.'

"Stan," she hesitantly went on, "I can only imagine how hard you worked. I'm sorry. I didn't mean to hurt you."

"Rita, its too late for this." I said. "What do you want?"

"I don't want this to be hanging between us." she replied, and in the tone of her voice I heard the spiritualist I had so liked the month before reappear.

'So this is how it will be.' I thought. 'We will discuss as equals this ugly matter.' and at that moment a profound calm descended. The sun, flooding through the truck windows, warmed the steering wheel, my lap, and the left side of my face. I turned off the engine and, in the ensuing quiet, the phone, pressed against my ear, commanded all my attention. My nervousness and anger melted away. What remained was a terrible clarity as sharp and dangerous as the bright noonday desert light.

"Rita," I said, "I can't recall ever being treated this badly. What were you thinking?"

"I wasn't."

"That's not true and you know it. You knew what you were doing. You just didn't care."

"But I do."

"You had every chance to call and make another appointment. Why didn't you call?"

"Well, David told me you were angry. I wanted to give you time to cool down."

"Rita, you didn't call because you didn't want to disturb your day off. No matter what I had done, it was not going to be important enough to get you out of bed. You didn't call because you didn't want to reschedule."

Silence.

"You had the morning to make it right. You had 3 hours to call, then put on some clothes and come to the studio. You knew this was your only opportunity to see these paintings. You knew that last month you'd encouraged me to do all this work. You knew that to now stand me up would be the worst kind of insult. But you did it anyway. Don't tell me you weren't thinking. You just didn't care."

"Stan, I'm sorry. I didn't want to deal with your anger."

"I'm not angry with you. After a short time, I wasn't angry with you yesterday. I'm terribly hurt and disappointed, and confused. What could I have done to deserve this treatment from you?"

"You know, Rita, I had an open house in the afternoon and everyone there knew what had happened. I wasn't walking around calling you ugly names. I wasn't speaking badly of you. I was simply stunned that you could be so cruel."

"I'm sorry. I didn't mean to hurt you."

"But you did. Rita, last month, when we had that

long visit, I found myself genuinely liking you. I actually thought you would make a good person to work with."

"I felt the same towards you, Stan."

"Then you pull this shit. Why did you turn around and treat me with such disrespect?"

"I didn't mean to. If I could take it back I would."

" ..... Rita, I don't know what else to say. Why are you calling me now? What do you want from me?"

"I want you to forgive me."

"Forgive you?"

"Yes, I want your forgiveness."

I could not find a handhold on the face of this cliff suddenly put before me.

"I don't know how you can ask that of me."

"Stan, I don't want you to leave with this between us."

"Rita, this comes at the worst possible time. I can't deal with this ....."

"I like you, Stan. I respect you. I want us to be friends."

"But we aren't friends, Rita. A friend would never treat a friend the way you've treated me."

"But I like you, Stan. This is poison. I don't want this hanging between us."

"You know, this is a difficult time for me." I replied cautiously. "I've given up my studio and I'm walking away from the only home I've known for 25 years. I feel as if nothing I've done has made a damn bit of difference to this community. I've never felt more vulnerable in my life. At one time I thought it was enough just to do the work well; that the work would bring an audience along in its wake and in that way I would have success. But every scrap of attention I've gotten in this town I've had to fight for. I've never had an ally I could count on. I've failed. And now, just at my lowest point, as I'm on my way out of town, you carelessly stab me in the back. You did it as if it were nothing. Just a flick of the wrist."

"This was not my intention."

"But there you have it, intended or no. All you've done is remind me how cruel this place can be and how little I matter. Now you ask me to forgive you, like that's simply there for me to grant. I can't."

Pleadingly she asked, "What can I do to make this right?"

"Nothing. It's too late. There's nothing you can do."

"There has to be."

"You had your chance. Now its literally too late. The paintings are in my truck. This is my last trip to storage. From here I leave town. What are you going to do, Rita, run down here and pretend to look at them in my dark storage shed? Represent me because you feel guilty? Of course not. It's too late to make this right."

"But I don't want us to part like this."

"Rita, you hurt me as badly as I've ever been hurt, and you did it because you just didn't care. And now you care only because of the consequences to yourself."

A small, strangled cry of frustration and grief came from the phone.

"Ah, God!" she said, her words strangled, dreading every moment of this. "At times like this I hate this business."

"I understand." I said reasonably. "But don't kid yourself. This isn't about the differences between artists and dealers. This is about people treating each other respectfully."

I had said all this with such calm and uncompromising clarity that now all I wanted was for this conversation to end. 'Let her walk away.' I thought. 'Neither of us need more of this.'

"Look, Rita, you don't need my absolution. You'll do just fine without it. You'll hang up the phone and go about your life like nothing's happened. And if there's a lesson for you in this then, that's terrific. Take it to heart and don't ever do this sort of thing to anyone else ever again. But don't ask me to accept your apology. There are some things you can't take back. Sometimes there are consequences."

"Isn't there anything, Stan? Just tell me what I can do."

"Its too late." I said. "If you want forgiveness, look to yourself. I don't forgive you, Rita. You don't deserve it."

"But, Stan, ..."

"What? What, Rita? What is there left to say?"

"Nothing, I guess."

"Then goodbye."

I sat there for a time in the warmth of the truck, my eyes closed to the sun. For months I had been traveling through treacherous waters, my calloused hands upon the oars of a clumsy boat. I had forced it, by sheer will, through rapids, clinging seaweed, and difficult tides to this moment. All resistance had suddenly disappeared and, released, I drifted effortlessly out onto the smooth mirrored surface of a still lake. In no direction could I see a shore.

Eighteen days later, I lay in the darkened bedroom of my friend's house, sirens sounding in the city about me, and realized, much to my surprise, the substantial personal price I have paid for my belief in the power of art in the world. I have exercised tremendous faith in art's ability to rescue me from my own personal demons. What if I've been wrong? All my life I have stayed focused on becoming a painter of substance. What if painting has no power to transform but is only a metaphor, a shadow of the real thing? What do I do with that?

I am at a turning point. I have no idea if I have been a great success or a total and utter failure. I don't know how to measure it. There have been such monumental successes, the film being only the most obvious and public of them, yet I find myself at this strange crossroad asking this most basic of questions, "If a tree falls in the forest.....?"

....

We spent Tuesday night in a redwoods grove. I love the fact that they call them groves; makes me feel like a hobbit.

....

Wednesday night I crashed on Damian and Kelly's couch in

Arcata. That afternoon, while waiting for Damian to get off work, I drove several miles, then hiked a short distance over a sand dune to discover one of the most spectacular beaches I have ever seen. An infinity of sand stretched off in each direction, eventually disappearing into moist atmospheres. Surf sliced the shore in progressively layered and constantly moving tears upon the water. Cool winds tossed my hair and blew my jacket open like a kite. The gearing in my head went 'click' 'click' as tumblers fell into place. An hour later, as I climbed the hill back to the truck, a large group of cottages appeared across the road and my heart jumped. If I could, I would gladly stay here a month.

So I drove around the neighborhood, talked with some residents and found all these cottages were owned by a lumber company and, "No, not a chance I could get one for just a month." Still, it's a place to which I might return.

It was terrific seeing Damian and meeting Kelly for the first time. For several years Damian was my studio assistant while he attended The College of Santa Fe. Now he has become a Rastafarian potter and my friend, a good man with a great laugh. The three of us spent the evening over beers, sitting at their rough kitchen table in their tiny house, a wood-burning stove warming the room. They are living their lives as exuberantly as a young couple with few resources can. Bless them both.

Since Arcata, I have kept to the coast, the sound of the surf a healing tonic to my sore spirit. I am staying an extra day in a hotel overlooking a beach in northern Oregon. Last night I fell into a dreamless sleep listening to the persistent murmur of the gentle surf filtering through the open patio door of my second-story room.

letter to a friend

Dear Trisha,

I am sitting in The Lodge Cafe in Dawson Creek, British Columbia. There is a sign as you enter town, 'You are at Mile 0 of the Alaskan Highway'. Perpetually muddy streets describe a town more on the frontiers of civilization than anywhere I have ever been. All around me are big men driving big trucks. Every door posts a sign, 'Please remove muddy boots before entering'. There was a black rubber mat inside the door to my motel room. Heavy blackout curtains tucked tightly around a constantly working heating-air conditioning unit left me with the distinct impression of being in a sleeping chamber carefully prepared to block out the perpetual light of summer or the relentless cold of winter. This town is industry. It is big hands handling hard steel in cold darkness. These people are roughnecks. They play and work hard, crashing through an unforgiving physical world with money to be made and a price to pay.

What am I doing here?!!!

....

Vancouver is an attractive city, though rather tame and composed. Its architecture is 60s modernism taken to its lofty, airy, most livable conclusion. The effect is that of small rectangles busily floating about in space like tiny pieces of some much larger puzzle. After a day of gallery-hopping, I had found nothing of interest and went to bed disappointed. In the morning, as I prepared to leave, I decided to check out Granville Island, the only part of town I had not been to. Much to my surprise I found two working printmaking co-ops, several galleries, an art college, and a foundry. I was stunned! It was very Canadian (meaning very civil and careful in the making) but very exciting. After good talks with several artists, I left feeling hopeful and interested again. I am surprised at how much I miss The Printmaking Center in Santa Fe. Its closing may be a much bigger part of my leaving than I had imagined. Wherever I land I am going to need a print studio and group of artists to share it with.

I took Route 99 North out of the city and gassed in Lillooet, a small mining town set into a cliff overlooking a most extraordinary canyon. I've never much liked the mountains, with their deep shadows capturing the daylight too late or losing it too early, but as I rounded the last hairpin turn, this place (a convergence of two rivers, each dropping down from vast high plateaus) opened onto a view of thousand-foot vertical stone cliffs lit by the late afternoon sun. Above these canyon walls rose row upon row of ever-greater mountains tumbling off into the distance. It was a space so perfectly described it could be held in the chest.

Somewhere around Williams Lake, the light became chrome. By Dawson Creek, the sun had not set at 10 PM. Dusk is lasting for hours.

....

In Port Charles I met a young woman. She was my waitress at a deserted restaurant the night before I caught the ferry to Vancouver Island. She could not have been more than 27. She had 3 children ages 11, 5, and 6 months. No husband. Her boyfriend had just moved 50 miles south, leaving her alone with the new baby. She had worked her way through college in Wisconsin getting a degree in studio art and had a particular affinity for printmaking. When I told her I was an artist she could hardly contain her enthusiasm, starved as she was for this thing she had felt for so passionately. There was hunger in her eyes for a conversation she'd not had in a long time. An admirable woman. My heart went out to her.

While driving through rural Canada, I have continued to catch glimpses of young girls, dressed as nicely as they can manage, some in high heels and dresses, pushing baby carriages down the gravely streets of these small isolated towns.

In Clinton I took Dixie for her evening walk up a dark street behind my motel and passed a dilapidated one-bedroom house. A 'For Sale' sign was posted in an unkempt front yard strewn with plastic Wal-mart baby toys. An open garage had no car in it. Through a curtain-less picture window, I saw a young woman sitting on a tattered and sagging couch in a room of empty and damaged walls lit by the stark yellow light of an unshaded lamp. Her attention was transfixed by a TV placed below the window I was looking through. I saw her vacuous face full on and wondered if she was there at all.

I have been seeing you, Trisha, twenty years younger, in each of these girls.

These are only instances, but they have strung together like odd misshapen pearls and have gotten me thinking of our last conversation which, for me, was about personal responsibility and the nature of reality. Your contention that each of us, consciously and subconsciously, choose every experience of our lives contradicts my own sense that we live in a world where innocent children are often born into cruelty and natural disasters reach out blindly to claim the lives of the unprepared.

I need to tell you before it's too late that, knowing something of your difficult childhood and the sexual abuse you endured, I have nothing but the deepest respect for your remarkable tenacity in refusing to be a victim. I understand what you have done. In assuming responsibility, even for your powerlessness, you have gained power over those people and events that sought to oppress you. As a child you stood in fields beneath the blazing summer sun and, like a tiny tree with your feet planted stubbornly in the earth, you indulged your overwhelming anger. You huddled alone on cold winter nights under blankets too thin to protect you from real and imagined monsters and made your bargains with God. By disrupting the flow of life's habitual behaviors you have steered yourself from the mundane currents of everyday existence. In your awakening you have created for yourself the opportunity to peal away those layers of childhood trauma to find the truth of your life. In viewing the child of your youth through the lens of time you have gained perspective and, with it, forgiveness, self love, and healing.

You own your life as well as anyone I have ever met, and you have been willing to do the work and pay whatever price that might exact. My deepest respects to you. Truly, my deepest respect.

Sometimes it is the hardest thing, to wake up from your own dream.

....

The last two nights were spent in motels so miserable I cannot begin to tell you. It has been a strange drive since Dawson Creek.

The Alcan Highway consists of hundreds of miles of scrub trees with moments of spectacular beauty, followed by hundreds more miles of mosquito-infested forest. It is five days of hard driving from its beginning to Anchorage. Northern Canadians are some of the most gracious and friendly people I have ever met, but those people on the highway are of a different sort, especially those in the small outposts. The people who inhabit these villages along the highway are there because there is a gas station or a campsite that needs a convenience store. For this meager reason, they have to prepare for the harshest of environments. I passed by a roadside restaurant today at the top of the Continental Divide. Standing next to this building was a two-story metal barn with wooden steps leading to a single door in its face, no windows, and above the door, painted in big red letters, the word HOTEL. I burst into laughter at the ridiculousness of It untIl it dawned on me that this actually serves as a rescue place for people stranded in blizzards. It has certainly saved lives.

I stayed in a motel in Watson Lake, "Gateway to the Yukon." To check in I had to walk a gauntlet of drunken natives chain-smoking cigarettes in the hallway while white men in hunting cloths watched television in the sparsely populated adjoining bar. A young girl who cleans rooms in the morning stood flirting with the concierge, a marginal character with a sharp wit and dangerous little mustache. With mud on the floor and the sun still out at 9 PM, it all seemed so sad, sleazy, and wasted. Of course, it was Friday night and the only party in town. There are some beautiful lakes and mountains, but to live here would be certain hell.

Today I found a B & B just outside Whitehorse. They've put us in a cabin in the woods just off a fair-sized lake. I am told Martha Stewart did her thing here. After the last few nights it feels like heaven.

It is 9:20 PM and a strong beam of sunlight is falling on the kitchen wall. Below this light is Dixie in her bed, looking up at me with a tired and confused expression. She knows this is not natural.

midnight at the Meckstroth's

I am sitting in a rocking chair before a wall of windows overlooking a small lake that Ray and a number of his neighbors use as a landing strip for their float planes. The still waters are reflecting a blood-red light from a sunset that has just happened, throwing all earthly forms into deep shadows of greenish black. From the red sunset, the sky transits to a silvery blue-gray light overhead. This they call dusk. It will last till sunrise, the light never leaving the sky. This is the view from JoAnne and Ray's second story living room. It is midnight at the Meckstroth's.

It is a week now since I arrived here, my body and spirit vibrating slightly from my month-long drive up the coast, and I have fallen into a comfortable rhythm set by my sister and her husband. They are hardworking people, keeping a large property with two log cabins that they rent during the summers. Ray has a plane, deep-sea fishing boat and another smaller boat for river fishing, a camper, snowmobiles for the winter, and an ATV for the summer. As well as the large well-constructed barn, which is his workshop, they have a two-car garage with extra freezers for the meat he brings home from his hunting trips. Ray retired last year and now spends his time working on the property or hunting and fishing. JoAnne still does a lot of traveling. When she is not traveling, she is keeping up with Ray here at the house, which she does very well.

JoAnne has shown me how to clean the cabins and we have begun the large project of landscaping the front yard; building a new walkway and walls, terracing a hillside, etc. It looks like this will keep us busy throughout the summer. I am enjoying the hard physical labor.

Ray has offered to fly me out to a cabin on the tundra where I might have a few days of complete solitude to fish and write. I also hope to go deep-sea fishing with him at some point. I am driving JoAnne to Anchorage tomorrow to catch a plane and returning with Diane and Mike's pop-up camper, which they have offered to sell to me. I plan to take it up north and see more of the country before too long.

Dixie has discovered doggy heaven. Sophie, JoAnne and Ray's 6-month-old Labradoodle, along with Molly, the neighbor's basset hound puppy, are keeping her busy. She has become the old lady of the group, not always having the tolerance to put up with all the youthful exuberance. Now a one-person dog, she's sticking close by when she can and worrying when I leave her behind. My grandnephew, Luke, and I went out in the rowboat a few days ago. Twenty yards out and here comes Dixie, paddling after us for all she's worth, until she had a change of heart, suddenly realizing how difficult it would be getting into the boat. It was an act of desperation, having never swum before. She has finally learned what Frisbees are for and so she is now catching them in the yard with the same serious abandon once reserved for sticks.

So, I find myself in Alaska. I have no idea what I am supposed to be doing here. Before leaving Santa Fe I remember saying," I just want to be surprised." I have not been surprised. I have driven many, many miles to get to this grounded, peaceful place but I don't know what I'm doing here.

The afternoon following my arrival I was laying on the boat deck in a recliner, the sun beating down on my upturned face. The dogs were scattered about me in various states of stupor. Sounds of wildlife and a breeze in the trees left me with a sudden and profound sense of stillness and I found myself silently crying, tears streaming down my sideburns and tickling my ears. I was crying for the losses I have suffered in the last few years and the innocence that has gone with them. And I was also crying with relief, joy, and thankfulness that there is still a place I can go on this earth where I will be accepted and loved. Eventually, and not all that long from now, I will need to return to the larger world to find my way. For now it is enough to be here in this place where I might catch my breath.

you have asked me what has transpired .....

Last night, over dinner, Ray suggested I have my paintings photographed and put on coffee mugs! I argued diplomatically that it might be a good idea but only if I were doing representational imagery. Ray very sincerely felt that it might be a good way to earn 40 bucks. I said, finally, "Well, Ray, I actually find the thought of my paintings on coffee mugs rather ... disturbing." At that moment, JoAnne burst into laughter at the two of us. Soon we were talking about people spilling their coffee turning the cups every which way, "Oh, maybe that's what he was thinking!" JoAnne was just hysterical. I almost peed my pants.

Since arriving in Alaska I have done a lot of sleeping, hard physical labor, and not much else. It's been a very restful time. In the moments when I have managed to remain still, close my eyes, and look inward, I have discovered a worn and tattered man gazing out from the other side of a dusty mirror. I am left with this raw, unseasoned reality.

You have asked me what has transpired to cause me to leave Santa Fe and, looking back on this journal, I realize that I have not broached the subject in print. I have not had the personal strength or clarity of distance to tackle the issues at hand. Last night I slept 11 hours, so here are the blows as best I can put them together.

As you know, my split with Liz after 10 years left me depressed and sorely disappointed. To see swept away that kind of deep rooted emotional investment is wrenching enough to make one question the permanence of everything. Only after a great deal of difficult personal work had I begun to find some renewed enthusiasm for life.

From the beginning, OFF THE MAP was a spectacular event. Standing with Campbell in an open field just west of the D.H. Lawrence Ranch, watching as a crew of workman planted in the ground the first post of what would, in three short weeks, become the artifice of the Groden's cabin, I told him, "What I have to lend this film is a sense of authenticity. Whatever the final movie looks like, Campbell, the paintings will be authentic works of art." Though I knew he did not understand the difference between a contrived and authentic painting, I remained confident. If I handled myself properly, the proof would manifest itself on the canvas and, in turn, in the film. From that single moment of personal commitment proceeded a chain of events, the nature of which reached far beyond my own imaginings. Each day, despite my maturity, their potency entered my consciousness and colored my expectations for the future.

The Future arrived with the premier of the film on March 3rd of 2005 at New York's Lincoln Center For The Performing Arts. The event included a one-man show of my paintings, also at Lincoln Center.

In the grip of a bitterly cold winter I had driven three days from New Mexico to New York, the bed of my pickup truck loaded with paintings. As I stood outside the theater's entrance the evening lights of New York danced with a vigorous energy in the crisp night air. For the last half hour celebrities had been arriving to walk the red carpet. Through a large window I watched as Joan Allen and Campbell Scott, both radiant and shinning, stood posing before posters of the film as they were showered in a halo of frenetic camera flashes.

"My God, this is a real premier, isn't it?" I said to George Van Buskirk, the producer, as he approached with his wife.

"You've never been to a premier?" he asked. "Not even on the west coast?"

"Come inside, Stan."

The lights had dimmed and brightened three times signaling everyone to be seated. I had somehow found my way into Campbell's seat in the very center of the theater. To my right sat Kevin Bacon and on my left sat Cora, Jim TrueFrost's wife, whom I had been talking with in the lobby. She had, somehow, arranged for my occupation of Campbell's seat. "He's too nervous to watch." she had told me. "He'll be pacing in the lobby."

On the stage Paul Cohen, the distributor, spoke first. Then George Van Buskirk gave a short speech and introduced Campbell who thanked the audience of 350 for coming. He told them a bit about the making of the film and the long journey to this night of its release.

"And I would like to especially thank Stan Berning." he continued. "He did all the paintings for the film. He has driven all the way from New Mexico to hang a show for us next door. You'll see his work later at the party. Without Stan, this film could not have been made." and with those last words he exited the stage.

Cora grabbed my arm in surprised excitement as I made some involuntary gesture in Campbell's direction, hands to heart, and sat there stunned by the unreasonably generous gift he had just given me. For a fleeting moment, as the house lights came down and I sat in the darkness coming to terms with the magnitude of this honor, I had the presence of mind to question the wisdom of embracing this prayer Campbell had placed so powerfully into the world.

'This is not my movie.' I thought. 'This is Campbell's film. Why would he give it to me like this?' But then, how could I refuse? The movie was now mine as well.

Two weeks later came The Santa Fe Art Institute's Santa Fe premier. The following week the Ohio premier was held in my home town of New Bremen, with opening night reserved for my immediate family. A showing of work at a Houston gallery concluded a month filled with memorable experiences.

What followed was a deafening silence, a thunderclap in reverse. For various reasons, the film, despite terrific reviews, got a poor release. At a time when I was struggling to recover from my breakup with Liz all illusions seemed to shatter like glass upon this stone of disappointment. I have made my living demanding the attention of others, by not "going quietly into the night". 'If something this fine and extraordinary can be ignored,' I thought, 'then I can only feel overwhelmed by the enormity of the task before me. I cannot do this alone. I have no help. I am helpless.'

Over the last 12 years I've had a good career but, in the last two, I have experienced a steady downturn in my income. In January of 2002, feeling that my spirit was about to snap like a brittle twig upon the linear studies of the previous 10 years, I made a dramatic artistic change to figurative abstraction. Despite the fact that I sensed a slowdown in the marketplace, I chose to act boldly in the interest of my spiritual health. Three months later the movie project came along which threw me deeply and completely into the new series. Most of my income that year came directly from the film project and I thought, 'I was right. I am in a downturn. But this film will open doors and get me over the hump, I'm sure.' Then it went unreleased for two years.

My income took hits from an economy in slowdown, a corporate market avoiding the appearance of excess, a society becoming more conservative (looking to familiar imagery for comfort after 9/11), and my own personal movement away from the familiar. The end result was the selling of my studio to get out from under a small mountain of debt.

Of course, the debt I found myself in was not insurmountable. I would have fought hard to keep my studio had I found Santa Fe a place where I could continue to prosper and grow. But it seemed my time there had finished. I could not find a decent gallery to represent me. The closing of The Printmaking Center at The College of Santa Fe left a surprising hole in my social and creative life while the personal changes I had undergone moved me further away from the community at large. I was already a stranger by the time I decided to leave. All this came about while I was doing some of the best paintings of my life.

Opening my heart to the world and having remarkable experiences with the fllm, family, and friends has been terrific. Evident in this new figurative abstraction is a blossoming of spirit; a reconnecting with my emotional self. These newest paintings have proven to be the perfect tool to employ towards the process of awakening, helping me to access the unconscious and work a kind of magic upon it. In my deepest despair I have feared the act of making art to be a pointless exercise in metaphor. Daring to question the very validity of the creative process has been more a measure of the depth of my personal sense of helplessness than an honest questioning of art's nature, which I know so well to be valid.

The helplessness I have been feeling is a result of my own heightened expectation of success. I thought through art I could take an audience of many to a place they had never been before and inspire them, as I am inspired, by the journey. What I lost sight of is the fact that all art depends, in equal parts, on artist and viewer. Painting, music, literature and, yes, even film are all experienced one soul at a time. Which leads me to ask, "Which is the greater gift, to compose the music or to listen with passionate attention?" An artist's power is granted to him by his audience. Of course, not everyone is going to appreciate it. Of course. I knew that. I knew all of this.

But all my life I've had such high hopes.

So, I have cashed out and left with a few dollars in my pocket, my dog unhappily ensconced in the back seat of my pickup truck, and gone in search of some answers.

During my drive up the coast I kept gazing off to the west into the great expanse of ocean, never detouring inland. It dawned on me last week it was not just the ocean's beauty that had me spellbound. Rather, the view allowed me to turn my back, both physically and psychically, on everything and everyone. Unknowingly, I have been in search of a substantial solitude.

I don't pretend for one moment to have the complete picture. The jury is still out. I think there are deep currents at work and I am seeing little more than the light's reflection on the water's surface. I am not running away from anything and so I might find myself back in Santa Fe. I am not in search of some romantic vision. I only want the truth. I don't think it is in my nature to be self-indulgent. I am simply working very hard to understand.

I don't know if we, as humans, have answers to all the questions we are capable of asking. Eventually it might simply come down to getting back to work. But I know in my heart it is not yet that time.

There is still a distance to go and I am thankful for the time and opportunity to journey.

a sojourn to Santa Fe, a cabin fire, and fishing trip

I am sitting here in the living room of a large log house that is rocking to and fro as if it were mounted on the deck of a large ship. The strangest feeling. The ground has been moving since I returned yesterday from a two-day ocean excursion. On Thursday I brought in a 50-pound halibut. That night I slept in the boat's cabin parked on a cold and rocky black sand beach in Homer. Waking early, I saw the full moon setting over a purple sea framed by the distant black, white-capped mountains which form the inlet we were sailing out of. This desolate spit of land is a fearsomely beautiful place, as is much of Alaska.

Friday afternoon we were coming in from a slow day of fishing, the sea as calm as glass, Ray's 22 foot boat charging through the water throwing foam into the air. My beard tasted of salt in the wind. The engine droned hypnotically through the fog of my tired stupor. Distant mountains were blue against a blue sky sitting upon a deeper blue sea. Everything was blue. Cotton clouds, drifting white above, served as context to the sun's silver light sparkling upon the wave tops in pinpoints of diamond brilliance or smeared buttery on the smooth rolling swells of tidal current.

A week earlier, on the night of my return from Santa Fe, one of JoAnne and Ray's two cabins burned, gutted by a fire that could have been much worse. At one point flames were pouring out an open door while one of their guests, wielding a garden hose, got his eyebrows singed closing that same door he had just opened. The guests lost everything inside. The fire department stayed with their investigators late into the evening. The guests were moved into the main house and I was moved into the camper for the remainder of the week. The fire changes everything and I have discussed with Jo and Ray leaving earlier than planned. I certainly don't wish to be in their way, but also I am feeling rested and stronger than I have in quite some time. The visit to Santa Fe helped.

My niece, Diane, works for Alaska Airlines and so, on my sisters suggestion, I was able to fly to New Mexico on standby tickets. In Santa Fe I discovered a small community of people with a shared interest that far outweighs their personal differences: an interest in creating art. Hanging out with Charles, Angela, Judy, Timothy, Trisha, Sandy, Michael, Elizabeth, Nancy, and Pilar felt so very comfortable. They are good people, all artists in their own right, whom I number as my friends. The city itself is a culturally rich environment even though it's feeling rather sad and depressed these days. It is packed with more potential than most anywhere I have been. Though I'm not ready to end my travels, it is good to know that Santa Fe remains a possibility.

As I type this entry I am parked at a roadside campground just north of Anchor Point with views of the North Pacific laid out before me. I am told it is the western-most point one can get to by car in all of North America. Today I visited galleries in Homer and found exactly what I had expected: eagles, bears, and fish. As I have known all along, this is not my land. For the last few days I have begun longing for the road, preferably at 60 miles an hour and heading south. After what has seemed like a long rest (thank you, dear sister) I am prepared to move on.

It has recently dawned on me that time may be running out for this journey. The trip to Santa Fe served to remind me that life continues on and will, sooner than later, demand my attention. A part of me worries over the cachet I am throwing away by leaving Santa Fe just at a time when the film is being accepted so enthusiastically. But as I cast my vision into the future I see several more months of travel. (If I were in Santa Fe I would be helplessly knocking on doors still closed to me.) I will take this time to decide what my future should look like and gather the courage to wish it into the world.

I am now in need of just one place to stay for a month or two, undisturbed. A remote location, a sketch pad, a journal, and my computer.

Perhaps Mexico.

deep water

The Alaskan Highway from Palmer to Whitehorse was more spectacular this time by. On my way north I was disappointed by how tame the drive was, but now that I know what to expect I've been able to simply enjoy its remarkable beauty.

Late on a Friday afternoon I decided to take Route 37, "The Glacier Highway", from Watson Lake (still a smelly little armpit of a town) down to Smithers (a perfectly lovely Canadian village) and Prince George beyond. I immediately found myself on a narrow, twisting, pothole-laden side road driving directly into the most majestic and intimidating mountains I had yet seen. Black storm clouds loomed ominously over this range which, I discovered later, literally tumbles off into the distance, unending. Two days of poised driving later, having navigated roads that at times became little more than a washboard gravel driveway traversing mountain passes that looked down onto the snow-covered peaks of adjacent mountains, I emerged to a place called Bell II, the beginning of civilization and decent roadway.

After spending the evening in Smithers, where I power-sprayed two inches of mud the consistency of cement off my truck and pop-up, I drove all day to arrive in Prince George, a day-and-a-half from the US border.

Towards the end of the fifth day of driving, I was physically and mentally done in. I was daydreaming, recalling a dinner out with my sister JoAnne, my nieces Michelle and Diane, and Diane's son Lukas. We were sitting around a large corner table in one of Soldotna's few good restaurants, the five of us laughing so hard Lukas was afraid they would throw us out. During a lull in our jocularity I said to my sister, "JoAnne, do you realize how important it has been for me to be here?" and as she nodded her head, yes, her mouth full of food, I said, "It's important for me to know that you know that I know just how singularly important this time has been." Diane hiccuped a laugh before realizing how serious the moment was. A minute later we were again driving customers out the door.

The next day I was saying how little I was looking forward to the drive back down to the lower 48 when JoAnne stated, with no guile, "It seems like an awfully long way to come, Stan, but I think maybe there was no place else on the planet you could have gone to get what you've gotten here." We discussed it no further, each of us understanding the other perfectly but, myself at least, unable to put it into words.

So, this day, five days out, I was driving, my mind muddled with fatigue from the terribly long and treacherous journey. As I daydreamed, my mind brushed lightly over those two conversations with my sister. I soon found myself struggling to find a word to describe the gift I had no word for; this thing I could not have found anywhere else on the planet. Over and over again my mind kept worrying the question then, baffled, it would retreat, keeping its distance as if from some deep water.

I recalled arriving at their home disheveled of spirit, disrespected and unwanted by my own community. Those people of Santa Fe that might have supported me had chosen instead to turn away. Worse than not understanding me, they had chosen not even to look. My own will had proved not enough. I had failed. Out of this failure, so complete and devastating, a covenant with my childhood self to believe in myself had been broken. The child of my youth had been lost. Cut adrift, I could not find my way back to him.

Traveling south, the late afternoon sun came dazzling through the trees to land upon the roadway in strobing pockets of light and shadow. My mind, in search of a word, again approached the dark water. But this time I thought, 'I wonder, if asked, what my sister would call it?' Suddenly, dredged from the very bottom of that deep black pool, came a guttural cry and wrenching volume of emotion as, with a jolt of startled recognition, my word for it broke through the water's surface like a bright orange balloon. As it burst in the air, luminous red letters left shimmering in space spelled HONOR.

"Oh my God! That's what I was there for! What a profound act! What a simple thing!"

My sister, ten years older than I, had been present as I dreamed the dreams of a baby. Over the years she had watched helplessly as that child was bent and twisted by the unpredictable winds of carnal life. Her faith had allowed her to love equally, and with full knowledge, both the awestruck child that still dwells at my core and the gnarled woody tree my worldly shape has become. By honoring me with her love and respect she had returned to me the child of my youth and truest self.

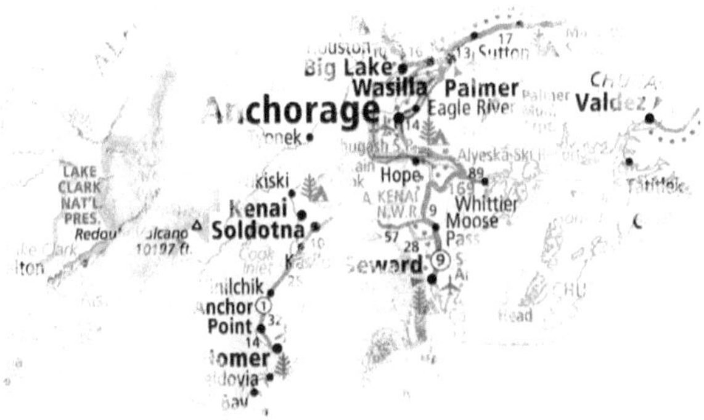

Big Lake
Sutton
Wasilla
Palmer
Valdez
Anchorage
Eagle River
Hope
Whittier
LAKE
CLARK
NAT'L
PRES.
Kenai
Soldotna
Moose
Pass
Seward
Point

Avalon, Salt Spring Island, Victoria, and a ferry ride

On the deck of the Ferry from Vancover to Salt Spring Island I met a dark haired, heavily tattooed young woman on her way to visit her brother. When he failed to meet her at the dock, I drove her over the narrow and winding tree lined roads to her brother's home. Located on the north tip of the island, the small, delicately proportioned Victorian house was built on a wooded hillside at the end of a long driveway. In the garden, wild with flowers, which surrounded the house, three-year-old twin girls ran naked and giggling in the water from their mother's garden hose. Barefoot in her t-shirt and shorts; her skin white and transparent in the late afternoon light, this pretty, slightly overweight woman looked upon her two children with a calm and self satisfied smile as she lightly splashed water at their feet. Through the trees, which climbed up the steep hillside above the house, sunlight fell in a dappled shower. For one surprised moment, quickly forgotten, as I gazed upon this idyllic scene (the gingerbread house with its white picket fence, the riotous garden and surrounding woods, these perfectly formed cherubs ecstatic with glee) my mind skipped with the realization that I had just walked into someone else's dream.

Her husband, a handsome man in his mid twenties, I immediately liked. A carpenter in his youthful prime, he carried with him the same weight of responsibility I have seen in my own older brother. After showing me the house, telling me the story of luck and chance surrounding it's purchase and pointing out all the flaws still needing to be fixed, he left for a baseball game. I walked him to his car and, as we stood there in the driveway, he asked me questions about my tent-camper, a thing he would like to buy for traveling with his family. In his practical manner sounded a note of hard won realism which plucked at my heart. I found myself liking him more with each passing minute. Upon his leaving, as we shook hands, I said, surprising even myself, "Its been an honor meeting you." After his distracted reply I stopped him and said, "No, I really mean it. Its been a real honor meeting you."

Surprised, he looked at me as if for the first time before saying, this time more carefully, "Yes, me too."

Having been invited for dinner, I sat on the porch surrounded by his sister, his wife, and two children. As I stared out over the garden, its riot of color now fallen into deep shadows created by the surrounding hill and woods, his wife began talking of how powerful she was at imagining herself into the world. With a gesture which took in all her surroundings she said, "I have brought this man, this house, these children to me. If you can imagine it, it can be brought to you and all that is brought to you is good." This she repeated several times. It was her mantra. "If it can be brought to you it is good. The secret to being good at this is to have no regrets." She had studied this philosophy with a famous new age teacher, she explained, and had taken to it like a fish to water. Her charming face smiled upon me like a gift. For a moment I felt sexually transfixed and utterly blessed.

But then she spoke an aside to the sister which became a conversation. Said without context, I was left scrambling to understand. "What was I thinking?" she said. "He was like an animal bringing all the animal out in me. It was crazy. We fucked like animals. We danced every night and he always had his arms around me, keeping me off balance. I couldn't get my balance back. But I know that what happened was necessary and good because I brought this to me as well. I know I hurt your brother but he has forgiven me. Will you?"

Soon after this she went to put the children to bed and the sister, leaning close in, told me the story. Her brother's wife had disappeared for two weeks, abandoning her husband and children while she ran about the island with another man. Now she was a few days back, begging forgiveness. Her husband, hurt and confused, no longer knew the woman. "Why did you tell me you loved me?" he had asked her. "If this is what you wanted then why did you ask for these children, this house, me?" He had decided to wait and see. "This is the mother of my children." he had told his sister. "What else can I do but give it time?"

As she returned to the table I found a curtain had been pulled aside. Disguised within her softly rounded face, sat far too angular of features . A splinter, lodged in the iris of her beautiful blue eye, once seen, could not be ignored. She was a woman of power yet morally bankrupt or, if one wished to be generous, dangerously - catastrophically confused. This creature did not know it yet, but she had broken herself badly and would, on her way down, break all these beautiful children of God.

The air grew cold and I grew restless. As I drove away in search of a place for the night, the thought came to me that it is not enough to know how to pray. Every wish comes with a corner, side, or back that cannot be seen. The world seemed suddenly full of dangerous children, too young to yet fear the consequences, recklessly imagining themselves into the world. And so I said my own prayer that somehow her husband might find honor and her innocent children safe haven.

....

On my way north, Salt Spring Island had been described to me as the Santa Fe of the Northwest, attracting artists and healers from around the world due to its unique geography. Floating upon a foundation of salt, somehow on this island off the coast of Vancouver the ionic poles reverse themselves. It is a lovely little place. I sense a certain pleasantly ajar undercurrent of confusion amongst the residents who seem, for the most part, genuine and sincere. Late on the day after my arrival, I got my hands on a guide for the island's Studio Tour. The disappointing array of mediocre crafts, unfortunately, colored everything.

Dinner that night at The Tree House Cafe featured live music played by ex-employees of the restaurant. The lead singer had the handsome and serious look of a pro about him until he smiled to show the worst teeth ever. All of them were down-dressed cool and not bad musicians. The audience was made up of mostly tourists from the mainland feeling not quite comfortable. Mixed in were the local 'truly cool' people. It would be hard to imagine cooler, the kind who seem to own the place just by showing up. The rich foreign girls were there as well, too sure of their own style not to overdress and showing too much hip and bust while sporting elaborate tattoos done by real artists. Their handsome young men sat alert at their sides. I've seen it all before and responded to it as I always have, with a bit of distance but also feeling comfortable and not at all excluded.

By mid-afternoon of the next day I'd done the 'world famous' fair and gotten a pretty good impression of what the island is about. The ionic poles may be reversed but they don't generate a kilowatt of truly creative energy. Yes, it's good there is a place on the planet that grows its vegetables in small, chemical-free gardens and still believes in animal husbandry and the barter system. But that does not create art. Tis' a sad bucolic state of affairs. How boring. But then later, sitting in this once-pasture-now- RV-Park in the hot afternoon sun, I quite effortlessly scrawled out a prayer for the 'place' I might be happy in (a beautiful geological setting; a spacious studio with proper light; a loving, supportive, and interesting woman; a receptive, supportive, enthusiastic gallery or two or three; a cozy home, warm in the winter and cool in the summer, with a yard, garden, and trees; a comfortable group of friends of intelligence and grace whom I can count on and who can count on me). Later still, I found myself doing my first watercolors in three months, rhythmic seascape poems. The sunset was complex with green, blue, and orange mixed from deep black to creamy white. So, I did not meet that truly fine artist. Nor did I encounter, as I had hoped, those enlightened individuals that might show me a spiritual path. Still, I did have a beautiful day. On this day that was enough.

The following morning I was up early. Over the fields a mist rose. Horses grazed in a neighboring pasture. A rooster clucked and crowed. A beautiful spot. Who cares?

....

Later the same day I spent five hours on the Victoria docks waiting to board the evening ferry for Port Angeles. The city streets and harbor walkways were lined with perfectly spaced hanging baskets of red flowers. I found their visual rhythm in careful syncopation with the human-scaled, seaport-inspired architecture of this very contemporary city. The warm, still air was disturbed only by the sound of cheering crowds drifting over the harbor from a banner strewn opposite shore. They were having sculling races. Finding a park with shade for Dixie, and later a restaurant with internet service, I spent the day sitting still, close to my dog, awaiting departure.

By 8 PM all had boarded and the ship's horn sounded. I was standing on deck, several stories above the water's surface, looking out over the harbor when the boat began to back out of its mooring. Suddenly the city that all day had lain quietly distant came to life in all its shimmering complexity. As angles shifted and turned in the pink evening light it dawned on me with surprising clarity how movement begets perspective. Through movement we discern the true shape of a thing.

As we powered out of their pristine harbor I turned to a couple standing next to me and said, "It's hard to imagine anything more civilized, isn't it?" I do very much like Canada.

....

The sun set as we moved into a dense fog bank. The sea, which had been like glass, turned violent with large swells. I found myself sitting in the cafeteria staring out the window at a wet black deck, white railing, and a tossing sea just beyond and below, appearing then disappearing with the roll of the ship. It was late in the sailing and the passengers had settled, many sleeping with their heads cupped in folded arms on the tables in front of them. A card game was in progress on the opposite side of the room. The ships engines thrummed hypnotically. With the fog had come cold and many wore sweaters, their hoods pulled up for warmth. Ugly yellow overhead lights illuminated the scene. I observed all this in the reflection of the darkened window I was resting my head against. It felt like forever since we had left Victoria, though in truth it had only been an hour.

I suddenly had the impression I was in a Polanski film, some sensual story of murder on the high seas. (There is a sordid seduction by some suicidal beauty involving a pistol and a paraplegic husband. I am caught up in a harrowing psychological adventure of someone else's creation.) Of course it was simply one of those moments created by the unfamiliar ambiance of a place. Still, at times like these, I am astonished by how far I am from the place I was three months ago. Who would have thought?

Be it traveling upon the earth, an object turned in the hand, or the turning of our own most intimate self, let's hope it's true that through movement we might discern the true shape of a thing.

"Take any space you want," he said.

Do you remember, Liz, the time I left your hanging bag behind on our car trip to San Francisco and for the next week you were dressed like a bag lady? Trouble often awaits those who fail to plan ahead. This story had to be told and you, of all my friends, are the most likely to appreciate its humor and irony. Still, it would be unfair to blame me for tonight's accommodations.

This morning Dixie and I were in an RV Park twenty five miles outside of Portland with a beautiful view of the Columbia River. My time there had been spent walking along the river's beach, doing watercolor sketches, and catching up with e-mail. Over breakfast I decided to head back down-river towards the coast, eventually stopping in Del Ray Beach (spectacular) and Tillamook Head. Along the way down Route A1A, I stopped at one campsite after another to find them all full. Ah yes, it's Saturday and the summer is in full swing! While taking a detour to Oceanside I glimpsed a run-down looking RV park off to one side. After Oceanside I stopped at a state park called Cape Mears, hoping it was a campsite but finding instead a lighthouse on breathtaking cliffs overlooking Three Arch Rocks. It was late in the day by the time I'd made the loop back to Tillamook and I found myself thinking, 'Perhaps this will take me back by that RV Park.' No sooner had I thought this than, sure enough, there it was.

Pulling into the drive I could see for the first time just how run-down the place was. Of the smattering of trailers, most appeared to have been parked for quite some time. A large cinderblock structure serving as a mechanic's shop had old junked cars scattered about it. An ancient Airstream trailer, up on blocks, was parked in front and sported a crudely painted sign over its door that read 'OFFICE'. Three goats came over to greet me as a tall lanky man in oil stained cloths, a three-day beard and very few teeth came walking around the corner of the building. He told me, "Yes, we have hookups and it's 15 bucks a night." I gave him 15 bucks and we stood for a moment talking about the two engines sitting on the floor of his garage and how he is putting one of them into that car over there, this as he pointed to a half-demolished Chevy painted in racing colors and a #12. "It's a Derby car." he told me. He, his wife, and kids do the Derby. "It's a family thing."

"Take any space you want," he said.

As I drove into the lot I became increasingly skeptical. An old woman in house slippers and a tattered purple bathrobe emerged from a smaller unpainted cinderblock building I could only assume to be the bathrooms. Throwing furtive glances in my direction, she shuffled as rapidly as she could across the weed infested field towards her trailer in hopes of not being caught out by the stranger pulling in. As I surveyed the possibilities I managed to find a spot between the only trailer that seemed passably well kept and a new travel home most likely occupied by people in the same position I was in. As I backed into the space, the more permanent neighbor came out to settle her dogs. One of them proceeded to follow Dixie around with the hair standing up on her back. Dixie, as always, handled the situation admirably.

Needing more boards to level off my tent camper, I returned to the garage. My host was impressed with Dixie, who quickly obeyed my command to 'stay' when she showed too much interest in the goats. (They moved off in a group to peer cautiously from behind a far corner of the building.) He seemed amicable to conversation until he discovered I originally came from Ohio, at which time his long boney head tilted back and off to the side as he looked down his nose at me, like a bad stage actor in a silent movie, with the most blatant and unguarded expression of suspicion. Surprised, I thought to myself, 'You don't trust me because I'm from OHIO?'

As I walked back to my camper with my arms full of greasy two-by-fours, a burly man in shorts and a dirty T-shirt came out from between two trailers and proceeded to question me about Dixie, making sure in his own mind that that dog would not be hanging out in his yard.

I eventually managed to get my camper set up in the dog-turd infested field and proceed to the bathrooms where... well, let's not go there. I mean, literally, let's not go there.

Sitting in my lawn chair outside my pop-up eating a sandwich I had bought along the way and watching the sun set over an adjacent bean field, I noticed Dixie staying unusually close, looking at me with a most anxious and bewildered expression as if to say, "Can we go now? Hey, let's go now." I soothed her, telling her it was all right, no one was going to hurt us and we would leave in the morning. She calmed right down. My dog often has better sense than I do which, in this instance, worries me greatly.

I have spent the evening in my trailer hardly daring to venture out. It is now time for bed. If you receive this e-mail it means I survived the night, without a shower.

dancing impossibly close to the edge

Nineteen days out of Soldotna on the second leg of this journey. Today was a long day. Two hundred miles down the coast of Oregon filled with vistas so spectacular my chest hurts from what I've seen.

From the balcony of my hotel room in Yachatz, I watched a woman walking along the beach soon after sunset. The tide had been out half an hour earlier but now it had begun to come in, filling the tide pools Dixie and I so recently had been walking through. Her solitary figure disappeared into the distance of the darkening beach. As I was ready to return to my room she appeared again, a tiny black figure in the distance outlined by the pale light reflecting on the ocean's surface from a dim dusk sky. In the darkness her indistinct form appeared impossibly frail and the sea took on the ominous danger of an unforgiving void. Out to the edge of the waves she walked, so impossibly far it appeared she was surrounded by the churning sea. My attention was so bent toward her that, for the longest time, all that was in the world was this frail spirit dancing on the edge of the abyss. I found myself fearfully willing her back. A few minutes later she was lost to the night, still dancing impossibly close to the edge, only now in complete darkness.

a mad rush down the coast

I am just outside San Diego camping on a bluff overlooking the ocean.

From San Francisco I have made a mad rush down the coast, driving the Coastal Highway all the way through Los Angeles as well, simply to do it. I had thought to turn inland to Palm Desert, then Phoenix and on to Santa Fe for a month of painting, but yesterday I decided to continue south. In part, I am afraid of losing momentum. In part, I still need time to travel. It has been in my thoughts from the very beginning to end this trip on a beach in Mexico. I would hate to end the journey prematurely.

Something happened to me on my return visit to San Francisco. Walking into Howard's studio was like walking into a familiar garden. (A good studio is as close to coming home as I am likely to get.) A large part of me wants to start painting again but my reconciliation with the events of the last few years, though emotionally felt, is only vaguely defined. I have seemingly separate thoughts about a vision of home, the nature of being an artist in today's world, and the giving and receiving of honor. These vague ideas need to somehow coalesce into a coherent vision of a future I can live in happily. It is time to come to terms with who I am personally, what my role is publicly, and what my life means spiritually. And it seems important to understand all this well enough to put into words.

So tomorrow I shall pass over into Mexico, for me uncharted and uncontemplated territory, in search of a safe, secluded beach where I can write and paint.

into Mexico

Two days ago I passed into Mexico, driving hard to get as deep into the country as possible. Now there is no easy turning back. On the second day I found myself quietly laughing, realizing that just weeks ago I was in Alaska and now, here I am in Mexico, having driven it all.

There is only one two-lane road running the length of this 800-mile peninsula. Narrow and dangerous, it winds through one small town after another. The towns themselves are like nothing I have any experience with. Haphazard storefronts, built of cinderblock and plywood, stand in the red dusty earth twenty feet back from the roadway. Outdoor markets and eateries bustle with people. Traffic is brisk and there is a sense of energy as people go about their business. Pickup trucks with 6, 8, even 10 men in the back are common. And then there's the man in his broad brimmed hat crouched alongside the road watching sheep grazing along the fence line. A cow got out on the road in front of me. As I stopped to allow a cowboy to chase it down he threw a rock at the departing steer's ass. By my frame of reference there is tremendous poverty here, but what I see is people living their lives with great energy and raw enthusiasm.

North of here, between the US border and Ensenada, is an odd juxtaposition of new Mexico and old. Californians are moving in by the droves building luxury houses they could not afford in The States. White-walled high-rises and pristine beach homes stand alongside rambling junkyards and slums where the poorest live in squalor. It is quite obscene, really.

On the first day, as I drove further south and the afternoon progressed, a golden reddish light infused the dust-covered trees of this rock-strewn desert country. I have passed through quite a number of military checkpoints by now, which make me truly nervous. What are they doing out here anyway? Thus far they have simply waved me through, but the open display of guns puts me on edge. One never knows what to expect, a nineteen-year-old cherub almost too polite for his own good or some tough little asshole pissed to be out in the hot sun and wanting an excuse to go off.

My first evening out, a twelve-year-old boy sold me a six-pack of beer. His mother, the owner of the grocery, had a beautiful and genuine smile. Dixie was happy to be in a motel room and I was happy to be paying only 30 dollars for it. Carlos, the concierge, lived in Denver for a time and is now staying in this small town for a woman, of course. Over a cigarette he told me about the town and some Americans who have built an airstrip on the mesa with the intent of building two golf courses and housing complexes.

At some point along the way I began telling the soldiers I was going to the coast of Punta Concepción, this simply because someone in San Diego told me the beaches there are beautiful. I am flying by the seat of my pants in a country whose language I do not know. I am not sure if my journey will end there or maybe continue on to the mainland and south to Acapulco. It's hard to imagine turning back, or negotiating again these same roads on my return. Lord, it's been a drive.

While working on the Off The Map project we came to a point where I had to do sketches intended to illustrate the film character's first efforts at drawing. Julie, my model, suggested I use my left hand and within moments I was completely unhinged. This morning, it happened again while ordering, then paying for breakfast. Fumbling with phrases like 'buenos dias' and becoming unglued because I couldn't figure out what bills to hand the cashier had me vibrating by the time I got in the truck. Then I proceeded to drive through some of the most spectacular desert I have ever seen. About the time my heart would begin to ache from so much of a thing, it would change, then change again. Outside of Catavina, I first drove into a region of burnt mesa the color of rust, then into a vast field of house-sized boulders, a giant Sequoia forest, white sand dunes offering distant glimpses of an elusive coastline, and finally a deep canyon pass opening onto the Golfo de California. All this time I had been handling the winding two-lane road built as narrowly as possible with no shoulder at all and oncoming traffic (what little there is) coming at me at 70 miles an hour.

I'd purchased Bob Dylan's No Direction Home, The Soundtrack from a Starbucks before leaving San Diego and was listening to it my first day out. Those incredible early folk songs have been an ideal soundtrack to this journey through third world villages of agricultural workers and poverty. Today, after several hours of hard driving, my heart aching from this overwhelming desert and rattled to the core by my fear of not being in control, I turned on the radio, forgetting the CD was still loaded, and it picked up where it had left off the day before with Dylan wailing to "A Hard Rains A-Gonna Fall". I had somehow never truly listened to it. I was hearing the words for the first time. And at the end when he seems to cry out from the very depths of his soul "... and I will know my song well before I sing it!" I just broke down.

It would be quite ironic to do all this driving (Santa Fe to San Francisco and Soldotna then back south to Salt Spring Island, Portland, and now all the way down the Baja California Sur) simply to find a beach. But without the journey it would have been some other beach, if only for the difference in the man standing there. Yet, despite all these travels, I know I will somehow disappoint myself by being the same person I have always been for, seriously, how much can we really hope to change?

On this trip I have shaken things up while doing what I have always done (spending hours in solitude, creating), only rather than painting I have been writing. I have taken the person that I have always been and dragged him across the globe in hopes of a transformation I knew from the beginning could only start from within. Somehow the white sand beach I am looking for could not be found until I discovered it first in my own mind and heart. Perhaps with these words I am coming close to it.

My sister sent me an e-mail my last night in San Diego. She said something to this effect. "Make a Birthday wish, my dear brother and friend. Make it for something beyond your own abilities, something only God can grant. From your crazy mad in love with Jesus sister! JoAnne" I wrote her back promising to make the wish, so here it is. "God, please, take me to that white sand beach, both in my head and heart and in the world."

Tonight I am on the east coast north of Punta Concepción in a lovely little casita by a river in Mulegé. Though the sun has set, my shirt is off as I sit at a large wooden table in the open air beneath a thatched cabana, sweating. A breeze is finally beginning to blow through the palm trees. Distant thunder has been threatening rain all day, but it's doubtful. The manager has told me all these places are for sale. The owners are taking RV lots and building little houses on them. They cost 80 thousand and my first thought was, ' What a steal.' It is going on everywhere, this rush for land.

Most of the people I've encountered speak little English and I
have started carrying around my faithful English/Spanish
dictionary. Still, I am ashamed that during all those years in New
Mexico I did not bother to learn the language. Obviously, I am
overwhelmed.

grace

Yesterday morning, as I loaded the truck, it dawned on me that perhaps I should stay a few days beneath this beautiful cabana. Here, on the river's edge, surrounded by ancient palm trees, I might rest for a while. But it was in my mind that this place was not my beach. Exhausted from the emotions of the day before, I had a stroke of inspired thought; a leap to the next place on this journey. But I had loaded my truck and so, rather than staying to write, I sat for a moment on a stone wall in the parking lot, jotting down some words before leaving. They were these, "About Art: Of this I know more and better than any other thing I know. I know that....."

Most of the two-hour drive from Mulegé to Ligui overlooks an expansive cove formed by the outcrop of a peninsula of pink, sandy-soiled, cactus-covered hills called the Punta Concepción. They are the most still and clear waters I have ever seen, part of an already placid Golfo de California. Their stillness I found disturbing. The small white sand beaches scattered among a coastline of dry grasses and cactus seemed of too human a scale and, though I thought to stop, I continued on, thinking surely there would be beaches of greater expanse and more majestic character further on.

Turning west from Ligui, I passed through a range of mountains called the Sierra de la Giganta and on to a plateau that ran straight and fast due west to Villa Insurgentes. Turning north on 53 towards Santo Domingo, I went in search of an isolated beach. Many miles down this rough secondary road I began to worry that I had taken a wrong turn. I seemed to be getting further away from gas, food, and water while seeing no sign of ocean, just the driest scrub cactus and no traffic. Could I be heading further into the interior? What if I had a flat tire, or two? And me completely unable to communicate with any person I am likely to find out here. Eventually I turned back and, once on the main road, decided to try San Carlos on Highway 22. The name was familiar and the map showed the road ending near the coast.

An hour and a half later I was passing beneath a toxic yellow cloud so dense it threw a shadow upon the roadway. Emerging from two tall smokestacks rising from a large blue power plant on the north edge of town, it drifted lazily south as far as the eye could see. It was late Sunday afternoon.

Suddenly the road was busy. A small bridge traversing a narrow canal cluttered with boats and tents was filled with young people laughing and joshing, many wet from swimming. I was an object of curiosity as I negotiated the bridge but in my rearview mirror I saw myself being quickly forgotten. Driving into town I was thinking, 'This can't be it.' but the road ended at the closed gate of an industrial-looking pier while the village stretched back east a bit on two or three dusty dirt roads. As I once again crossed the bridge I caught a glimpse of a beautiful 14-year-old Hispanic girl. Tanned, dark-eyed, and lush of figure, she looked up smiling as she pulled away from the grip of a young boy of the same age, wrestling the way children that age do. Moments later a man in his early 30's drove by with his radio blasting, the huge smile on his face showing numerous silver fillings. All this energy! All this human beauty! All this juice for life in a factory town! I thought it was ugly. I thought it was inspired. I thought, "I will never know these people until I know their language." As I passed back under the toxic cloud a whiff actually caught in my nostrils and stung me.

Late in the day, I was setting up my camper in a deserted RV park in Constitución run by a friendly, hardworking Scandinavian couple in their early 60's when one of their dogs attacked Dixie. The man reached in to pull the dogs apart and was bitten twice on his left arm and hand. He came away bleeding badly! I was stunned, and he wanted a cigarette. His wife, who all this time had been in the empty swimming pool with a broom and dustpan, was cheerful. "No, No, don't you worry now. Is not your fault. You see that little female there? We just had her fixed but she still in her last heat, you know that smell, and the black dog protects her. You don't worry. Is not your fault." The place was a hundred degrees with no breeze and I was sweating profusely by the time I finished setting up. With all the canvas down on my tent camper I could feel no movement of air. As night fell I turned on my reading light and the bugs came to visit. By bedtime, I had done all the killing I could, but the restroom, with its light left on, had begun to look like a sanctuary for every kind of exotic bug. (This is why that lizard continues scurrying behind the toilet. It's like shooting fish in a barrel.) "Your dog sleeps inside with you?" she had asked. "I walk my dogs late at night so they won't see your dog, yes?"

It was very late. Not a wisp of air was moving. Dixie, panting profusely, was stuck on the hot floor of the pop-up. I was sitting on the edge of my bed, naked, sweating, and far too uncomfortable to sleep when I heard a rustling of animals outside my tent. When I turned on the overhead light, I found the female (a cute little dog who seemed to be forever smiling) standing patiently on my door mat, waiting for Dixie, while the black dog furiously humped her from behind. "Get!" I cried and went back to bed too tired to find any humor in it.

The next morning I managed to break camp before the heat set in. Still, by 9 AM, I was checking my e-mail at an internet cafe, sweating. I decided to again try Route 53. It should only be an hour away and it sure looked like there must be a great beach there. I took the same rough highway back to the place I had reached the day before and half a mile beyond found a sign for Santo Domingo. This area is flat desert with dusty gray sand that stays in the air as a powder and clings to everything. Seemingly far beyond the irrigated fields just 10 miles away, it is scrub desert. Vultures have made huge nests atop the electrical poles that stretch straight and unbroken off into the distance.

Santo Domingo is a village with a school, pool hall, bar and restaurant, and a small church. The streets are all dirt but the main road through town is divided by a median of trees and baseball-size stones painted white. The pool hall has no doors. Much of the glass in the school's windows has been replaced by plywood boards. But the church is well tended and the restaurant newly painted. A young man was wetting down the dirt in front of the restaurant as I pulled up to ask directions. Our exchange did not go well. I don't believe he had ever seen a gringo looking for a place to camp and I most certainly did not know better. Finally we mutually gave up with an exchange of smiles and I continued down the road toward what I imagined must be the ocean. Passing the local graveyard and several little ranches clustered together in a compound, I crossed a narrow cattle guard and drove on for several miles down a dirt lane running parallel to the sea but never offering access. As I again began feeling out of my depth, I stopped to check the map one more time and saw, lying 20 feet away, the carcass of a calf, its skin draped over a skeleton empty of flesh or gut. I decided it was probably time to turn back. Driving through town on my way back to the highway, an old man in a cowboy hat and a clean white shirt waved to me from the open doorway of a one-room shack I had taken to be abandoned. My God, what a place this is.

Heading back to Villa Insurgentes with the intention of driving on to Cabo San Lucas just so I could say, "Yes, I did all of the California Baja," a wave of fatigue hit. OK, enough is enough. Turning back inland, my heart set on Mulegé and praying that it would still be there for me, I found myself contemplating the difficulty of living a graceful life. It seems all my life I have been asking for grace, then pulling it about like a dog on a chain. And now I sit here, this whole year, daring to be disappointed, as if Grace has let me down. What a putz. What a sorry, road-sore putz I am.

I have rented the same cabana in Mulegé, this time for a week.

I pray for the return of grace.

about art

So, what do I know for sure?

I know I am a painter. I know on some levels I live my life quite courageously, while on other levels I am a coward. I know that, as an artist, I have never feared failure, but of late I have come to fear disappointment. I know I have suffered from sadness all my life. I know, at this very moment, I am indulging that sadness, as surely as I always have, turning my natural seriousness into art in the hope of elevating it to a thing greater than the petulant pout of a 15-year-old boy.

Over many years of work I have come to believe that painting is a process of transformation. Art, at its least, mirrors the internal dialog of one's life, but it will also inspire, direct, and inform one's process. Art's true power comes from its ability to surprise, to turn down unexpected paths, sometimes despite the protests of the artist creating the work. In these moments of surprise, which can be charged with fear or exultation, the process of image-building becomes a process of reshaping our internal selves. At times, after long periods of intense work, I have looked inward and sensed an actual reshaping of the space within my chest where I imagine my spirit to reside. I have believed wholeheartedly, all my life, in this process and its power.

We-- meaning we artists--begin life wanting to be rock stars. As a young man I wanted to get laid, be worshiped and given money and drugs; but most of all I wanted to be a part of history. It is the way aspiring artists are motivated as the hormones race through their young bodies. There are many ways to dream oneself through the world, but this is very much the artist's way: to dream of changing the world by changing the world's perception of itself, working from the spirit out but expressing and living this process through the physical medium of paint, sculpture, music, or literature.

Here is the rub. For all these many years, attached to my belief in the power of art, I have nursed an adolescent's desire for fame and fortune which, surprisingly enough, I never came to question as an adult. This desire for prestige led me to the irrational belief that, following rapidly on the heels of artistic success would come social beatification.

I have been a foolish, foolish man.

Upon looking back, it seems the irrationality of expecting society's praises for what is, essentially, a spiritual endeavor has stood behind a curtain, stage left, like an undertaker in a black suit whose eyes I would forever refused to meet, while my belief in the world as a just and benevolent place remained so integral to the very spirit of my deception that I never entertained the possibility of being wrong. I have cloaked this irrational thought in a stubbornly obtuse denial. Of course, this is the rational progression of events: First fearless dedication involving years of work, followed by an explosion of inspired thought, and finally the welcoming arms of an appreciative and slightly overwhelmed audience. Stan, shame on you. People are born, have children, grow old and die in hovels with more dignity than you can imagine from your vantage point inside your foolish quest for love through achievement.

God, this hurts!

As I have said before, I have been suffering a huge

disappointment born of unreasonable expectation.

Over the years, I have met many artists who have dreamed this dream. It truly is the artist's way. I am thrilled beyond words by the enthusiasm of the young. Envious of their journey only just begun, I never fail to say a prayer for their safe passage. In the eyes of elderly artists I sometimes find that glimmer of joy for the journey they have made and the remarkable things they have seen, but usually these are women who have had children and lives beyond the paint. The men, now they are often a different story.

Many, some of the best, have broken their backs on terrible disillusion. As a consequence of poor business decisions, artistic wrong turns, or simply poor luck, they have gone unrewarded despite having made an admirable journey consisting of real contributions. Faced with the public failure of their stubborn quest for an uncompromising vision, they have found in their bitter disappointment only the room to be bitter back.

This end is what I have feared for myself. It is why I am sitting here at this table in the sweltering heat placing these words upon my computer screen, dropping these thoughts into the waters of the world. I am looking for salvation from a poisonous fate. I am claiming my right to a life better, more admirable, and more humane than the death of a bitter old man. It is my birthright to dream my own dream, and I choose not to dream that one!

THERE, IT IS DONE!

There is a secret we artists share. All the dancers and musicians, the poets and painters, all the good ones know this secret and I will tell it to the world right now. Art is about sex. When it is not about sex it is about the painful absence of sex. The energy we call upon is sex. The path we walk is sex. All we fear to look at and all we perceive as truth is sex. When you listen to a great singer doing an inspired aria, precise notes dancing and tumbling about as you are transported away by the music, that is sex.

There are men who will have museums named after them, great beasts all, faithful to their own character. But these are men whose lives have landed upon a fortuitous thread of human time. We must all understand that at birth we fall from the sky like flakes of snow to find our bodies moist and waiting. The only choice we have in this world is to live life fully and with grace, or not.

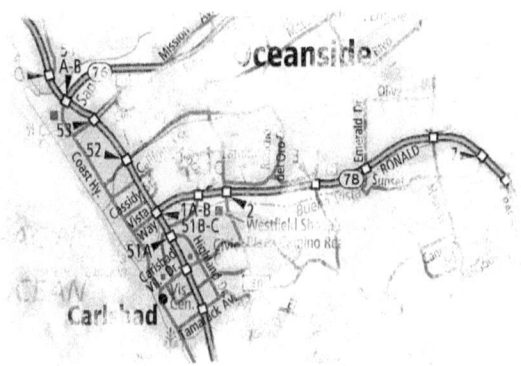

the escaped prisoner story

I am in Mulegé (pronounced moo-la-hay) which is on the eastern coast of the Baja de California. It feels like a safe haven after so much driving. I am not sure if I have ever experienced a greater heat than in this place. It is a beautiful spot in an oasis of palm trees alongside a river that empties into the Golfo de California a quarter mile away. If the breeze stirs there is some relief. Inside my little cinderblock hut beneath a large thatched cabana, the air conditioner rages and just manages to keep it tolerable. Still, I am out here in this heat, shirtless and sweating, loving the novelty of sitting at a kitchen table in the open air as if it were my office.

I have spent the last three days writing and have managed, I think, to come to terms with my life. That is, in itself, an amazing thing to say, but I believe it to be true. The most dangerous of secrets and most damaging of flaws are those hidden, in plain view, from ourselves. Here in Mulegé I have looked behind my own curtain.

After hour upon hour of staring at this computer screen, pulling as if from my gut the most painful of truths, I looked up to see a world cleansed. I had the supreme feeling of having redeemed myself. I decided to go looking for a beach. Having packed my watercolors, books, and towels, I motioned Dixie into the back seat of my pickup. As I was pulling out of the parking lot I decided it was too early and still too hot for the beach. I turned right rather than left.

It was again a culture shock driving through town. Not having the language is as disconcerting as having an arm suddenly missing. For this entire trip through Mexico, the experience has kept me off balance, which is, of course, exactly what I have needed.

I suddenly saw a sign for the Mulegé Mission.

It is a beautiful place, 300 years old last year. Built on the top of a hill overlooking the town and its forest of palm trees, it has doors situated to capture the ocean breezes so that its modestly sized stone interior seems the coolest place on earth. There is a wooden sculpture of a bleeding Christ. He stands, sadly gazing down, his arms bound before him, draped in a real red robe with real human hair stirring in the breeze. Spooky.

As I walked up the steps a tall hispanic man in his early twenties approached me. His head was shaved and his arms were covered with gang tattoos. His white t-shirt and jeans were covered in dust and recently sweat-stained, as if he had just run across miles of desert in the midday heat. He drank greedily from a half-empty plastic milk jug filled with water. His eyes were deep brown pools. His voice was profoundly calm.

When he realized I spoke no Spanish he began speaking perfect English. He was from Long Beach, California, he told me. There was a well-dressed, soft-spoken man and his young son there as well whom I assumed correctly to be the caretaker. These two spoke no English and so the man with the jug started serving as my translator. Soon after, he asked if I was heading north. He was in need of a ride.
"No", I said. "I am staying here in Mulege."
"Well then, can you give me a ride to the gas station on the outskirts of town? I have been walking in this heat and I'm broke, a stranger in Mexico trying to get home."
Some subtle cue in his demeanor suggested I should not refuse

him, while his calm voice and beautiful eyes put me at a certain ease. After viewing the mission I found myself in an alcove off the main chapel buying souvenir cards by way of thanks. I noted him crouched in the shadows against the room's cool stone walls, his now nearly empty water jug in hand,. He had not taken his eyes off me since my arrival. I had become the object of his obsessive attention and I resented it.

Accompanying me to the truck, he began this dialogue: "I don't say this to make you nervous, but you know in the United States kidnapping is a crime, but it isn't here."
I interrupted him to say, "Does this mean I shouldn't let you in my truck?"
"No, no, my point is my wife put me in this drug rehab center down here and now they won't let me out. They are terrible down here. They tie you up and beat you and there are no laws about the way they can treat you." As he said this he held his hands up to show me wrists that had been scraped raw of flesh.
I had been clearing off the front seat, putting everything in the bed of the truck. I made a big show when he began to climb in before me. "No, no! Not yet! My dog's in there. She'll be fine once I'm inside." then pretended to calm Dixie as the two of us climbed in. With her alert face at eye level just inches between us she looked formidable. As I had hoped, she would give him another thing to worry about.
As we proceeded to drive down the hill and through the town in search of the highway he continued to embellish the story about his wife, asking me to let him know when we got near the gas station in town because, "This is where they will be on the lookout for me."
With some consternation I told him, "I don't know where the gas station in town is."

"Well, I'm really nervous as you might think. This has been such an ordeal." Suddenly he was talking like some perfect sociopath!

I began thinking, 'Oh shit, have I gotten myself into it now.'

I continued to drive slowly, very slowly, through the small village when suddenly he yelled, "Shit!" and slumped down onto the floorboard of the truck, pressing as close to the door as he could get. "That's them!" he cried. "That's them right over there! Did they see me? Huh, did they see me?!"

As I cruised, ever so slowly, up onto Highway 1, I saw in my rear view mirror three men with handmade wooden nightsticks get off the porch they were sitting on, climb into a beat up Toyota pickup truck, and follow us.

"Oh man, are they following us? Did they see me? What's happening, man?"

As the Toyota made a move to pull up beside me I pulled my truck over into the dirt saying to the man on the floor, "Yea, they saw you, man. It's over."

"You're not going to let them take me are you?" he pleaded. "They're not real cops!"

"It's too late. It's out of my hands." and with that they threw open the door and my passenger submissively fell out, surrendering himself in the universal manner of prisoners: wrists held together, shoulders hunched forward, and head downcast. Like an animal awaiting the next blow from an unpredictable master, all signs of willfulness evaporated as he stood in this position surrounded by the men with their poised clubs.

As I sat there waiting to be pulled out next, they spirited him into the back seat of their pickup truck. One of the men turned to me and said, in English, "Thank you." I suddenly realized that the mission's caretaker had been on the phone the moment we left. How else would they know that I spoke no Spanish or be so sure that I had no intent to be part of an escape. All this happened--from my arrival at the mission to the departure of the prisoner--in the span of no more than 15 minutes.

I turned around and headed back the way I'd come, shaken and wondering what lesson to take away from this one. The only thing I can come up with is, "Yeah, have your moments of euphoric revelation, Stan, but then come back to earth quickly because at any moment life can reach out and bite you in the ass."

I spent the evening over one of the best meals I've ever had at a restaurant called Mike's Place. The Cuban owner, Mike, spoke perfect English. He introduced me to a couple from California who had just bought a house in the community I am staying in. We talked over sunset and drinks.
Marilyn asked me during dinner, "So what do you do during the day?" as if to say, "OK, you're here for a week so, what is your job here?"
I made a bit of fun of her for the way she had asked the question, it sounding so very American. "Well, do I have to do something?" But then I confided that I am keeping an online journal and all the writing is keeping me busy.
Steve then interjected, "And now you have the escaped prisoner story to tell."
"Yes." I replied, "It seems my whole journey has gone this way. I can barely keep up."

He doesn't know the half of it. Here in Mulegé I have finally faced the demon of my discontent.

....

It is 7 AM. After staying up late last night to put down the story of the escaped prisoner, I went to bed but could not sleep. Realizing how close I had come to a miserable fate has left me feeling vulnerable. While doing so much writing, it has been a challenge not to turn all my experiences into metaphors, searching for meanings where perhaps there are none. But this, this was extraordinary. Yesterday I brushed up against a young, very beautiful and bad man living his own fateful life and with one false move could have lost my own. Seldom do we have the opportunity to come so close to a disastrous fate and emerge unscathed. I won't soon forget his beautiful eyes, his desperate pleading, or that cool perfect English he was able to call up that was so deliberately meant to soothe and make me feel he was like me, not like them.

Last night I had dreams of negotiating traffic badly (cars pulling into wrong lanes, not being able to stop at lights, other men leaning out their windows cursing, confusion and fear of crashing). This morning I awoke to nervousness in my chest and a sense that danger awaits me here in this strange country. Dixie is behaving badly, her ears pulled back in an anxious fashion I don't like, her attention never leaving me, eyes alert and cautious. I think she senses my rattled discomfort. I think also the heat has almost done her in.

But I look around and see a vaulted cabana surrounded by huge palm trees, their fronds stirred lazily by an almost nonexistent breeze. I hear workmen sawing and hammering across the way. They are building new houses. The houses are being bought by Americans, of course. The people seem hardworking, industrious, and big-hearted when given the opportunity, but I am the white guy and I am left wondering what they think of me. I know much of the trepidation and frustration I feel is due to the lack of language. Life here is cheap. The most beautiful roadside stops are littered with trash. Broken guard rails are left as obstacles along the roadside long after families have planted their crosses and shrines to loved ones who have died there. The beaches are lovely crystal clear lagoons, as still somehow, as the desert that surrounds them.

Two days later:

Yesterday I paid another visit to the mission carrying a note I had spent an hour composing from my English/Spanish dictionary, thanking the caretaker for yesterday's help and asking permission to sit in his church for a while. As I was driving through town, school let out. The girls in their clean white dresses and knee socks and the boys in their white shirts and khaki pants seemed like bouquets of white flowers strewn through the streets. The caretaker was not there and the mission was closed, but I hung out on the hilltop anyway, sitting for a while in the shade of the mission's east wall, paying my respects. From the mission's vantage point high above the town you can see Mulege laid out before you. It is a desert oasis on the edge of an ocean. A forest of palm trees hides, then reveals, a brackish river winding through a valley of low-lying pink desert hills. Towards the horizon these hills rise up in folds of progressively lighter pastel ridges, the jagged contours of which seem torn from sheets of fine paper. Four prehistoric birds (long, sleek, and pointed, with huge wingspans) effortlessly rode the sea breezes that rocked and clattered among the palms and stirred my now much longer hair.

Later I went to a beach and swam in salt water the temperature of my skin. Lying on my back with my ears submerged, I listened to my own breathing while a lone cloud passed overhead and cooled my face. I thought of nothing, only vaguely aware of Dixie, who sat on shore watching curiously.

After dinner on the beach, I came back to my cabana and made my prayer for the future. I doubt it is a prayer that will save me any pain. It is merely the best prayer I can make at this time. So here it is. It is done with the sincerest of intentions and hope for a long and worthwhile life.

what I choose

So, what do I choose?

I choose to live in the path of grace wherever and however I may find it and to whatever end it may lead.

And what do I wish it to look like?

I think it is best to go back to Salt Spring Island for this: " a beautiful geological setting; a spacious studio with proper light; a loving, supportive, and interesting woman; a receptive, supportive, and enthusiastic gallery or two, or three; a cozy home, warm in the winter and cool in the summer, with a yard, garden, and trees; a comfortable group of friends of intelligence and grace whom I can count on and who can count on me"

And I would wish for one more thing before I die. The opportunity and courage to love fearlessly one last time.

This is the wish I put out into the world.

Amen

taking leave

Four months of traveling has culminated in these last few days in Mulegé, channeling a spirit, facing a demon, making a prayer. It's been a harrowing journey.

After the last of my notes had been made, emotions subsiding in my chest, I took a short walk up the river. Three doors up from my casita, a small group of men (part of the crew building the new houses in this compound) were getting blow jobs from a couple of used-looking whores in the back yard of an unoccupied house. When I realized what was going on I was stunned. How vulgar and sad! I learned from my neighbor over dinner last night that these men are from down south, living in tents at the other end of the property. The landowner, who is not well liked in town, brought them in because he could get them for ten dollars a day, while the locals would expect thirteen. They work twelve-hour days six days a week for those ten dollars. It is all so beyond my experience. How can I presume to judge their character, given those circumstances?

After dinner at an open-air restaurant, the parking lot sky was filled with stars. Ellen, a lovely, intelligent woman and recent transplant from San Francisco, asked if I had seen the sea at night. I confessed I had not. So a group of us drove out to the beach and stood in the light surf swishing our hands in the sandy bottom as sparks of luminescent organisms flickered about our fingers. The stars blazed above us while the sea's horizon disappeared into a gray indistinct darkness.

Last night I woke again from dreams. I was buying a ticket for a passage home and I stood in line at a table as officials assisted a group behind me. As a man in this group pushed rudely by I lost my temper. The anger brought me awake. My mind refused to settle as I lay there, the air conditioner roar oscillating with my vibrating nerves. This morning I was again dreaming. I had just walked through a confusing conflagration of stairs in some large rambling beach house and, as I walked down the last flight of steps to a street in Santa Fe (Canyon Road but covered in dirt), I viewed a number of familiar art dealers scurrying about in frenetic occupation, their arms full of papers. As I stood by the curbside, my head down, engrossed in the reading of a map, I slowly became aware of being surrounded by a large group of people standing uncomfortably close. My first thought was, 'Isn't that nice. All these people just want to be close to me.' When I looked up I found, much to my embarrassment and amusement, that I was standing in front of the side door to their van, which was open. They were waiting for me to move so they could climb in!

Mulegé has done a number on me. It seems when I was born a tuning fork was struck and all my life it has vibrated at different frequencies as I moved across the earth, grew tall and grew old. Here in this place it's as if a large glass bowl was placed over this vibrating fork, amplifying and reflecting back its pitch and timbre.

It now dawns on me that, while I remained vulnerable in my great disappointment, a piece of OFF THE MAP's sadness and tragedy glommed onto my psyche. I have carried with me not just my own sadness but the distinct texture of the films sad melancholy as well. For all this time I have been unable to break its spell.

On my last visit to San Francisco, Joyce claimed that on my way up the coast I had told her I was no longer an artist. It is hard to imagine me saying such a thing. Perhaps she interpreted that from some other thing I'd said, or perhaps I said it. Something in me had certainly been broken. In retrospect, I now understand how this small bleached bone near the center of my soul had broken so badly I could not bear to look at it. In Alaska, the Meckstroth's, through hard physical labor, unconditional love, and much laughter set the bone in place. It will now take time to heal.

Once this entry is finished, I will go into my blessedly cool cinderblock hut and begin packing. I still have the treacherous drive back up the Baja and many more miles from San Diego to Santa Fe, but the journey I came for is ended. The rest is postscript. I find myself still crying at the drop of a hat, but I trust this will end once I get out from under this bowl. Or maybe it will go on forever. I don't know. To whatever needs to happen now, I surrender.

Today I drove thirty miles north to Santa Rosalia to pay for my tourist visa, which had to be done at a bank. I spent the morning walking through town, buying fruit and melons and having breakfast at a restaurant overlooking the ocean. Later I drove thirty miles south to Playa Riquesón, the southernmost beach of the Punta Concepción, and did my watercolor, swam, and laid upon the beach watching with amusement Dixie's arduous and futile stalking of a heron.

Though I still fear the hard cynicism of the larger world (the stone upon which I have fallen to hurt myself) it is time for me to return. All the broken pieces must now be picked up and put back together, or cleared away. Everyone, I am coming home a different man, amazed that I, who had always hoped to change the world, managed only to change himself.

a shrine of lilies

At 3 AM, having arrived in San Diego to find the coast's motels booked, I decided to sleep in the truck. I found a parking lot at the end of a back street in Oceanside and slept with my window open to the surf. Two hours later I awoke to the dawn coming foggy and slow and took Dixie for a walk a mile down the beach and back. A woman had slept the night on the beach up against the sandy sea wall cliff. Closer to the water she had built a fragile shrine of lilies and had etched a name in the sand before it which I respectfully refused to read.

To my sleep-deprived and travel-addled mind, the thought arose that I had still not found my white sand beach. I had been given the opportunity to see it in my head and heart, but where was it in the world? Before leaving Mulege I had thought that, yes, I had still not seen it there before me, but I had let go of the thought with some relief. A part of me feared that to arrive at that beach might be my death and, if that were the case, I would just as soon wait a while longer for that part of my wish to be fulfilled. But no sooner had I stopped again to ask the question than the realization quickly followed and dropped me to my knees.

IT IS ALL ONE SEA!

On my long coastal journey, from the prehistoric black stone beaches of Homer to the iridescent pearl-like shores of the Punta Concepción, I had experienced the sea in its many personae. In search of my one beach, I had not realized all these beaches were but glimpses of a greater body.

Late in my journey I had discovered that, even when I had lost sight of it, my true-self had always been with me in my head and heart. Now the realization came which shook the very fabric of the atmosphere around me. The beach I had traveled so far to find had been right there in front of me the whole time.

my borrowed place

I have been up since 4 AM, awakened by a pack of coyotes killing prey not far from the house. They howl to call one another but mew in this strange tongue when they are killing. The weather reports are predicting scattered snow showers in the higher elevations, while outside my door a light rain is falling. When I turn on the patio lights, the flagstones and rough furniture are slick with wet, brightly illuminated. Ten yards out the light abruptly loses its power, overwhelmed by the deep blackness of a fenced but still wild desert.

If it clears, a rich gray of no discernible depth or distance will replace night's dome of blackness and stars as the earth turns towards day. Above distant mountains to the west, still submerged in a pond of featureless blue and watery shadow, pinkish red will infuse the atmosphere. Above this line of energetic light the sky will take on the resounding blue of the coming day.

I will sit here at my kitchen table looking through the west-facing glass French doors and watch the sun's light make its first appearance, falling upon the Jemez Range fifty miles away. Over the course of fifteen minutes this line of light will drop from mountain to plateau to desert floor and finally reach the scrub grass just beyond my patio where an hour before stood only inky and dangerous blackness.

This is my borrowed place.

Painting again, I am forever reminded there are no guarantees. Paintings die in my hands, only some to be resurrected. The act of painting offers no surety. It is not a process of absolutes.

I know these paintings now for what they are. They are magic incantations, holy prayers meant to conjure from my deepest self those small significant truths that, taken together, form an understanding of what it means to be human upon this earth. And they are my personal attempt to transcend the human condition by discovering within the context of each frame a place of grace. In this respect, they represent the best of what I am, often despite what I am: a flawed man continually in the process of becoming.

But finally, they are no more than pigment on canvas and scraps of paper. Most will surely be lost to fire or neglect. They are only buildings to be blown down with the next big wind, stories to be buried in libraries too deep to be found. What remains of importance is no more or less than the precious and eternal moment in which the thing can be done, and the doing of it. And so the journey begins anew.....

With some relief I now leave this business of writing behind and return to my desert studio.

About Art: Of this I know more and better than any other thing I know. I know that....

postscript

Last night I attended my Wednesday night drawing group. After 10 minutes of quick sketches the long pose began. The model had used this pose before and I had seen it from exactly the same position. Suddenly the thought of sitting there for 3 hours became overwhelming. I closed my eyes for a full minute, resting, but when I looked again she was still there. No one was going to ask her to change position. My head hurt. I left early.

I have been getting eye-aches from these extended periods of drawing, something I do not recall having experienced before, and a different kind of ache located behind the eyes and deeper in the brain tissue at an overworked muscle or synapses stimulated to its limit. This has only happened twice. Each time I've had to leave the session and rest for 24 hours.

Much of the work consists of quick pen and ink line drawings on moleskin paper. In three to four sessions I can fill up a sketchbook of sixty pages with these quick contour drawings, most of which have multiple overlapping drawings on each page. These then get cut out and mounted to paper or panel, creating a grid pattern of line drawings over which the pastel or oil stick work is done. These black contour drawings, peaking out from behind the colorful oil pastels, add an extra level of energy even while the eye has a tendency to ignore the blacks in favor of the color work.

The grid pattern formed by the moleskin pages, laid one next to the other on the surface of the paper, is so subtle it disappears as the oil pastel drawing is put down. But I am convinced of its profound influence on the finished image. Subconsciously it adds a structural underpinning that helps to hold the work together even while it disappears. The yellow tint of the moleskin paper, mounted to a heavier paper of white, supplies the image with a natural border which is visually just powerful enough to contain the edges. It allows me to leave those edges unfinished which adds to the image's overall energy. I also like the fact that all these beautiful drawings lay hidden beneath. It is like a secret gift.

Thus far the color work has been... unusual. Last week, at the Friday morning John Sloan Drawing Group, Bob, a rather well known art critic in his time, stopped by, as he often does, to visit. Late in the session he stood behind me as I drew. I was working with a great sense of frustration on an oil pastel. It's designer colors of pale golds, yellows, yellow greens and dark olives had brought it to a far too quick and comfortable conclusion. As I was in the process of asking myself how I was going to get out of this box he interrupted my thoughts with a joke about capturing the model's likeness, then quickly followed with, "All joking aside, Stan, I like the drawing very much, but what more can one say about it?"
After genuinely thanking him for his compliment I returned to my work. 'Well,' I thought, 'one could say, It is familiar ground and, as such, far too self conscious. One could say, It is a child with a plain face only a designer could love. One could say, Those days of being pleased with an image because it is simply beautiful are long over, Bob. I am trying to save my life here.'

In an effort to discover whatever new ground might be available to me, I am deliberately avoiding those easy and familiar resolves that have served me so well in the past. The results are, at the moment, a bit chaotic as I use unusual combinations of colors in seemingly nonsensical layers; that is, until late in the process when it becomes necessary to impose my will. By then I hope some new, surprising, and enlightening things have happened.

After another day of drawing and painting, I stood looking into an oil pastel of lush oranges, pinks, and whites as aggressive and juicy as any De Kooning. It is as if I had somehow gotten the fingers of my hands wedged between two parts of the painting process that, up till that moment, had fit together seamlessly and, like two flaps of skin, pulled them apart to expose the gut.

This morning the thought came to me, 'What will this work look like in a year?' I know better than to think I can accurately visualize these paintings into the future. Inevitably, some unexpected insight or turn, made upon the head of a needle, will redirect the process. From a series of small and large aesthetic decisions will arise a cascade of unforeseen consequences and I will be left scrambling to keep up with the materials as they lead me to places far beyond my own meager ability to imagine. It is in the volatile nature of these physical materials of paint and brush, solvent and roller, that I am granted the opportunity to express, in action and metaphor, the most basic of human truths: through acts of choice we create the world, even while the world remains an unpredictable and dangerous place.

After wandering the dark streets of an unknown city I found myself in the large room of a larger house. Sitting upon a couch, I watched as Marguerite walked by. She was in deep conversation with two others about a movie she was acting in. They were discussing tomorrow's scene. I watched this sensual older woman from beneath a blanket I had pulled partially over my head to disguise myself. I was a guest here, but I seemed to have been invited by no one.

Lying to my left beneath the blanket -- shoulder to shoulder, foot to foot -- was a young woman. Her right hand rested firmly on my crotch. My left hand lay lightly upon her cotton underwear, soft and thin beneath my finger tips. As I thought, 'She is too young for this old man.' her pelvis began to rock against my hand.

Having been awakened from a stunned sleep by the sound of clattering dishes, I stood at a kitchen sink, half conscious, washing my glass, while a woman of very solid presence loaded the dishwasher at my side. "May I stay the night?" I said. She smiled radiantly, grateful for having been asked, and told me, "Of course you're welcome to stay."
"So, you're making a movie?" I asked.
"Yes." she replied.
"I love the movies." I said. "They take all these elements, these different parts, and wrap them into a single larger thing."
As I spoke I fell slowly backwards onto the couch which had been carefully prepared with pillows and blankets. Perfectly shaped to fit my body, they formed a kind of soft cocoon about me. Tears welled in my eyes as I continued. "I feel so badly for all those artists lost in the larger process of the film." A perfect feather of sadness brushed my chest. "I feel so badly for all those artists down through the generations that have failed."

Each night, ambiguity and non-sequential time are superimposed upon the linear experience of our waking life. We dream. We daydream. Our minds drift. We fantasize, project, and imagine.

> *I sat at a long table, absorbed in my work. A man walked through the door and announced excitedly, "He has arrived!", then stepped aside. As my gaze was torn reluctantly away from the computer screen a handsome man in his early twenties, with close cropped hair and a plaid shirt tucked conservatively into starched new blue jeans, walked through the door. He came straight to me and, as we embraced, my hand grasped the back of his neck. Beneath my hand his neck was as hard with muscle as a tree trunk. It crossed my mind to wonder, 'What am I going to do with this kid?' before holding him at arms length and saying, "My God, look at you. How you've grown!"*

From this intermingling of dream and waking states the fabric of human experience is woven.

> *Picking clumps of matted hair from the surrounding bramble bushes, I walked through an open field. Placing this wild bear-hair in a plastic garbage bag was a form of protection, a talisman of sorts against danger. Small brown bears lumbered around me, circulating among people who also walked about in the field. One bear sat upon my foot, leaning against my leg as Dixie sometimes*

does. I awoke to a sense of benevolent danger.

Should that fabric become a silk robe or suit of nails depends upon a series of choices, the consequences of which we cannot predict, made as we attempt to disentangle these dream visions and reconcile them with the realities of our waking lives. Herein lies the source of our free will and creative power.

All those years ago, as a child sprawled upon my parents living room floor copying pictures onto brown paper bags, then as a young and clueless adult aspiring to paint just one image that might change the world, and later, as a striving man building his career, one prayer was spoken and acted upon every day amidst all the prayers that came and went. "May I be a good painter; an authentic artist; a true believer in the power of art in the world." As I stand now amidst the beauty and ruin of my imperfect life I am comforted by the knowledge that this prayer is, along with all its unintended consequences, what I have imagined into the world.

Painting again, I have regained my perspective and found, buried within these pages and from a surprising source, the fundamental truth I had forgotten. On the north tip of Salt Spring Island, a broken witch will forever sweep her hands in a gesture encompassing all her domain and utter a truth, the importance of which she will not fully grasp till the end of her days.

"The secret to being good at this is to have no regrets."

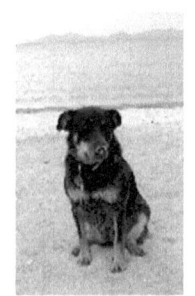

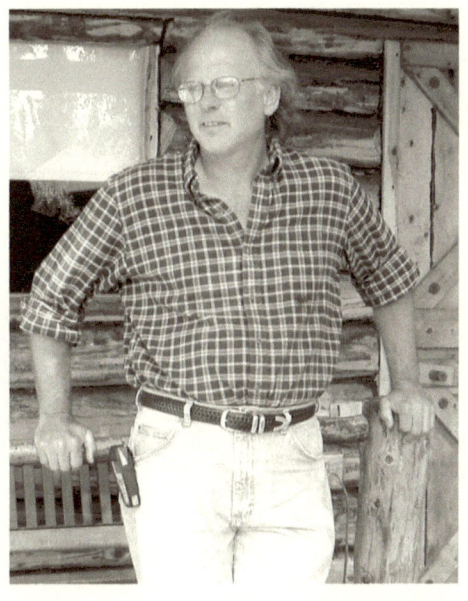

www.stanberning.com
www.aboutartbook.com

letter to the artist Elly Prestegard / Norway
1/2/09

Dear Elly,

Thank you for your thoughtful response to my difficult manuscript.

I am concerned that my story deals with a theme most artists, myself included, would prefer to set aside. Though it is a challenging story, I've no desire to undermine the reader's faith in the power of the creative process. I hope this experience of mine might help others, faced with similar disillusionment, to deal with their disappointment from a place of spiritual strength.

You've asked me, "How have I changed since the beginning of this journey?" I am not quite sure how to answer this.

Last week I received a preliminary copy of 'about art'. It was a powerful experience. This manuscript, which I have worked so diligently to complete, had become an object I could hold in my hand. Leafing through it and finding it all there, I realized that the texture of the last few years -- all the suffering and searching, the depression and dreamlike detachment -- was captured and contained between its pages. Later that day I felt it psychically break off from me. From my right shoulder the bubble of it detached from the rest of my body. I stood there holding all the disappointment of the last few years, now a separate thing, in my hand.

'OK', I thought. 'So now I am fully returned to the world.' My next thought was, 'What next?'

As artists we work with one foot in the physical world and the other in the realm of spirit while using a language based in the elements of music and metaphor. It now seems to me we should not be so despondent when the larger world fails in its rush to embrace our personal song. If the desire for recognition is an integral part of your dream (as was mine) and if that desire is then left unfulfilled or, when fulfilled is found to be something entirely unexpected, one does not throw away the whole of the dream. One simply changes that part which created such disappointment. All this time, Elly, through all my soul searching, I have continued painting.

In the context of painting I have been subverting the role expectation and ambition play in the creative process. During this last year a stack of paintings has grown upon my studio table, unphotographed. I finish a piece and throw it on the pile, unstudied. I refuse to lend these objects undo importance by my attention to them. They are simply artifacts, remnants of the real work of remaining engaged in the process.

I am still not sure what significance these paintings I create have in the larger world, but I have come to believe that what I believe does not matter for the world will make of them what it will. For now it is enough to embrace the creative process without expectation as I refuse to allow my happiness to be dependent on the whims of strangers. In this respect, my future now becomes a new story. I am determined it will not be a tragic one.

I know we will probably never meet face to face, Elly, but thank you so much for reading the manuscript. And thank you for your spirit and the spirit of your work. You have the right idea, I think. Embracing both the child and adult in each of us; sending honor, respect, and kindness into the world; doing all this with a sense of joyful play, a keen eye, and a generous heart. All this is good work worthy of a person's life.

It seems the best we can do is go about touching other's hearts one soul at a time. In the process, if we can be kind, we can build about us a tolerable world.

Affectionately yours,

Stan Berning

www.ingramcontent.com/pod-product-compliance
Lightning Source LLC
Chambersburg PA
CBHW030812180526
45163CB00003B/1243